Cloud-Dwellers of the Himalayas
The Bhotia

by Windsor Chorlton
and the Editors of Time-Life Books
Photographs by Nik Wheeler

PEOPLES OF THE WILD · TIME-LIFE BOOKS · AMSTERDAM

TIME-LIFE BOOKS

European Editor: Kit van Tulleken
Design Director: Louis Klein
Photography Director: Pamela Marke
Chief of Research: Vanessa Kramer
Planning Director: Alan Lothian
Chief Sub-Editor: Ilse Gray

PEOPLES OF THE WILD
Series Editor: Gillian Boucher
Head Researcher: Jackie Matthews
Picture Editor: Jeanne Griffiths
Series Designer: Rick Bowring
Series Co-ordinator: Elizabeth Jones

Editorial Staff for *Cloud-Dwellers of the Himalayas*
Text Editor: Louise Earwaker
Staff Writer: Deborah Thompson
Researcher: Judy Perle
Designer: Zaki Elia
Sub-Editor: Sally Rowland
Proofreader: Judith Heaton
Design Assistant: Paul Reeves

Editorial Production
Chief: Ellen Brush
Quality Control: Douglas Whitworth
Traffic Co-ordinators: Jane Lillicrap, Linda Mallett
Picture Co-ordinator: Rebecca Read
Art Department: Janet Matthew
Editorial Department: Debra Lelliott, Sylvia Osborne

Published by Time-Life Books B.V., Ottho Heldringstraat 5, 1066 AZ Amsterdam.

ISBN 7054 0705 5

TIME-LIFE is a trademark of Time Incorporated U.S.A.

Contents

The Author

Windsor Chorlton was born in the north of England in 1948. He worked for Time-Life Books as a senior editor for six years, before leaving to become a full-time freelance writer and wildlife photographer. Since 1973, he has spent a part of each year with the Berbers of Morocco, while studying the natural history of the High Atlas mountains.

The Photographer

Nik Wheeler is an English-born photographer based in Los Angeles. In 1967 he went to Vietnam as a combat photographer, and during the 1970s covered international events in the Middle East and elsewhere for *Time*, *Newsweek* and other journals. He is a correspondent for the Black Star agency, and has published several travel books, including two on Iraq and one on China.

The Volume Consultants

Professor Christoph von Fürer-Haimendorf has 45 years' experience of anthropological fieldwork in India and Nepal. Born in Austria in 1909, he studied Anthropology in Vienna and in London, where he now lives. In 1951 he became Professor of Asian Anthropology at London University, and until 1976 was head of the Anthropology and Sociology Department in the School of Oriental and African Studies, London. He has published the results of his extensive research in numerous books and papers.

Charlotte Hardman, who was born in London in 1949, studied Social Anthropology at the universities of Sussex and Oxford, and at the School of Oriental and African Studies in London. She first visited the Himalayas in 1968, and from 1976 to 1979 spent three years in Nepal doing field research among various Himalayan groups. During the same period she acted as consultant and translator for a German television film team, and she collaborated on an international project on the status of women in Nepal.

Dr. Michael Aris is a Research Fellow in Oriental Studies at Wolfson College, Oxford. After graduating in Modern History he spent five years in the Kingdom of Bhutan in the employment of the royal family and government. He is the author of *Bhutan: the Early History of a Himalayan Kingdom*. In 1979 he convened in Oxford the International Seminar on Tibetan Studies. He has travelled widely in the Himalayas and Tibet.

The Series Consultant

Malcolm McLeod, Keeper of Ethnography at the British Museum, was born in Edinburgh. After studying History and Social Anthropology at Oxford, he undertook research in Africa, concentrating on the Asante region and other areas of Ghana. He has taught in the Sociology Department of the University of Ghana and at Cambridge, and is the author of a book on the Asante.

Introduction

All along the southern fringes of Tibet, overshadowed by the soaring peaks of the Himalayas, dwell people whose way of life continues almost untouched by the outside world. The Bhotia graze herds of yaks on the mountain pastures and eke out what living they can from the thin soil. In winter, when snow covers their stone villages, they migrate to lowland areas to trade their yak products for grain. The homes of the 400,000 Bhotia—narrow, lofty valleys in Nepal and the lands to west and east—are isolated by mountain ranges and gorges cut by forest rivers, so that each community has evolved individual customs. But they share an ancestral home in Tibet, from whence they derive their language and culture, their Buddhist religion, their colourful homespun dress and their diet.

Their strongly independent lifestyle, and their ties with mysterious Tibet, made the Bhotia a certain choice for the *Peoples of the Wild* series. Deciding which Bhotia community to visit was more difficult; the most fascinating culturally were among the least accessible. With the advice of Professor Christoph von Fürer-Haimendorf, an expert on the Bhotia who has spent many years in Nepal, Time-Life settled on the two villages in the Nar-Phu valley in the extreme north of central Nepal, about 100 miles from Kathmandu as the crow flies. Although within reasonable reach of the country's capital, the villages were only miles from the Tibetan border, and so out-of-the-way that few had entered from outside the region. A team of four flew to the capital. With Professor Haimendorf were author Windsor Chorlton and photographer Nik Wheeler, both seasoned travellers, and anthropologist Charlotte Hardman, a fluent speaker of Nepali.

One major obstacle lay before the team: the problem of access. Much of Nepal's border region has been restricted territory since the Chinese invasion of Tibet in 1959; and no foreigner had been allowed to enter the Nar-Phu valley in more than 20 years. But the King of Nepal knew and admired Professor Haimendorf's work, and His Majesty's approval of the project brought the necessary permits. The journey was a strenuous 11-day walk that could only be undertaken with a small army of porters carrying equipment and provisions, and four Sherpa guides to lead the way.

Weary and suffering from the bitter Himalayan climate and the high altitude, the team arrived in Nar just in time to witness an extraordinary exorcism ceremony. They saw the hazards faced by herdsmen alone in the mountains with their yaks; later, they journeyed to Phu at the far end of the valley, and visited the camps of refugee Tibetan nomads. The team were impressed by the openness and generosity of all their Bhotia hosts—people whose independence and resourcefulness have enabled them to rise above the hardships imposed by one of the severest environments on earth.

The Editors

Built on a sheltered slope on the western side of the valley, the sunlit village of Nar looks down on terraced fields dusted with spring snow. By early afternoon, Nar will be deep in the shadow of the mountain behind.

crossed over the border into Nepal and made the mountains their base. To avoid provoking the Chinese, the Nepalese government all but closed the border with Tibet, thus barring the Bhotia from their usual northward trading route. Many communities, therefore, were forced to change drastically their trading patterns.

The people we chose to visit had been much less affected than most by the political upheavals. From their home in the Nar-Phu valley, in the very north of Manang District, they could cross into Tibet only with difficulty over a pass so tortuous that it is not shown on any map. Thus they had never become dependent on the trade in salt. For as long as they have inhabited the valley, yak herding has been the mainstay of their livelihood.

Two villages lie within the valley's length. The larger is Nar, "the place of the blue sheep", named after the wild sheep with blue-grey fleece that still roam the area. The second and more northerly village is aptly named Phu, "the head of the valley". Both are built above the tree line, on the upper limits of cultivation. At lower altitudes in the steep valley are other settlements where the villages cultivate a few fields, and where they retreat to when snow completely cuts off Nar and Phu during the depths of winter.

This much we had learnt from a book, published in 1961, by the British Tibetologist David Snellgrove and from more recent reports by a Nepalese anthropologist. When we arrived in Kathmandu, however, we had no prior assurance that we would be able to follow those writers to Nar and Phu. Because the two villages are situated in the sensitive border area, foreigners are not normally allowed to visit them. We therefore applied for special permits, fearing that we might be in for a long wait. Fortunately, Christoph's studies of Himalayan communities were well known to the King of Nepal, who found time in a crowded schedule to give him an audience; the leave we were seeking was granted. We were the first foreigners in over 20 years to be allowed to enter the Nar-Phu valley.

There was no road to our destination, 100 miles north-west of Kathmandu. We decided to drive west as far along our route as a Land Rover could get—to Turture, a village in lowland Nepal's Lamjung District—and then strike northwards on foot. We would need to take far more equipment than we could carry ourselves. Camping gear, clothes for the sub-zero temperatures and 500 rolls of film for Nik's cameras added up to quite a weight, but the main item would have to be food: the Bhotia would have none to spare for us at the end of their long winter.

In the end, our party numbered 34. The logistic problems of moving men and equipment were handled by four Sherpas. Ang Nuri, the leader of our team, was the veteran of five Himalayan climbing expeditions. He had survived an avalanche that swept away his camp on Annapurna II and had reached 26,000 feet on Lhotse, one of Everest's fearsome neighbours.

We had a cook—a member of the Rai tribe who live on the edge of Sherpa territory—who possessed the uncertain temperament of many great chefs but none of the talent, and two Tibetan interpreters, Yonden Lama and his girlfriend, a professional Tibetan dancer called Lhamo. Yonden had been

Crowding one of the muddy lanes between the sheer stone walls of Nar's houses, three yaks follow their owners towards the fields; two of them will be harnessed to a plough by means of the yoke that the woman carries balanced across her back-basket. Besides serving as draught and pack animals, yaks provide the villagers with milk and wool.

Himalayan Outposts

The homeland of the Bhotia follows the arc of the high Himalayas along the borderlands of Nepal and Tibet, extending some distance beyond Nepal's eastern and western boundaries. Occupying mountain valleys more than 10,000 feet above sea level, the scattered Bhotia settlements are isolated from one another by deep river gorges and snow-covered massifs.

The arrow on the map below marks the approximate location of the Nar-Phu valley in the far north of Nepal, home of the two Bhotia communities described in this book, and gives the orientation of the perspective view on the right.

The villages of Nar and Phu lie above the tree line in a cold and arid zone. The settlements of Meta, Chaku and Kyang, at slightly lower altitudes, provide temporary winter refuges for the villagers.

From Kathmandu, the most direct overland route to the Nar-Phu valley follows the course of the Marsyandi river, through the lush Himalayan foothills (foreground) and round the eastern end of the Annapurna range. From Kupar, precipitous trails wind up to Nar and Phu. A high pass leads northwards out of the valley to Tibet; another pass links Nar with Manang and other Bhotia villages in the valley behind Annapurna.

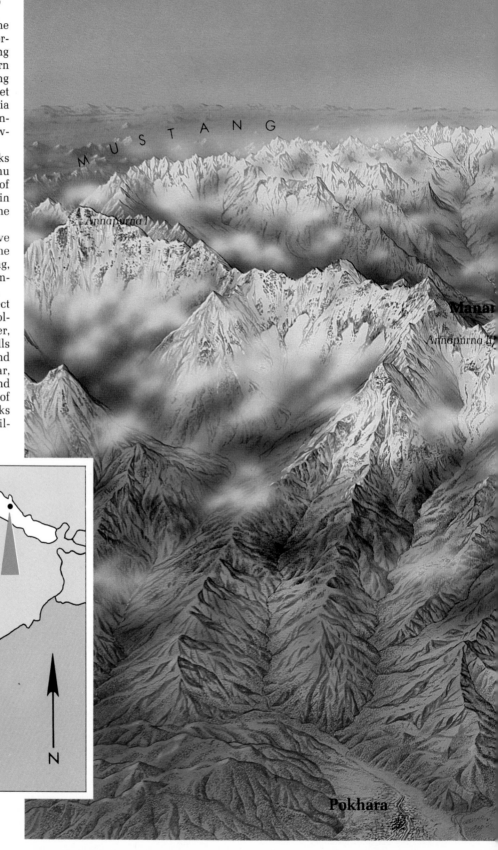

T I B E T

Phu

Kyang

Kang Guru

Chaku

Nar

Pisang Peak

Meta

Annapurna IV

Pisang

Annapurna II

Kupar

Chame

Thonje

Lamjung Himal

Turture

MANANG DISTRICT

raga

LAMJUNG DISTRICT

born in a Tibetan village, but in 1959, when he was four years old, he had moved with his family to Nepal. In his adopted country, Yonden was taught the rituals and precepts of Tibetan Buddhism by his grandfather, and the young man's understanding of religious custom was to prove vital to the success of the expedition.

And then there were the porters—23 of them, men and women, each carrying a 60-pound load in a straw basket that was secured by a broad strap passed around the forehead. They were a fair cross-section of the diverse ethnic groups that live in Nepal.

While we were still completing our preparations in Kathmandu, the guides and porters set out two days ahead for Turture. When we arrived in the Land Rover, our camp was being set up under the Sherpas' direction on the outskirts of the village.

That night, as we sweated in sub-tropical heat, the land of the Bhotia seemed very far away. Moths as big as my fist crashed into our hurricane lamp and fireflies pulsed in the darkness to the electric rasp of crickets. During the night, violet sheets of lightning rippled over the hills, and at six o'clock I awoke in a pool of rainwater to a morning that was already hot. But winter, I was to find, was only 11-days' walk away.

Our route lay upstream along the Marsyandi river which, for the first two days of our journey, ran broad and strong through the forested foothills of the Himalayas. Buffaloes peered up in brutish contentment from mud wallows near the banks. The path led through patches of lush forest, where pheasants with plumage as bright as enamel burst out of the undergrowth and gauzy butterflies glided through the humid air. Every mile or so we passed through hamlets of thatched wattle-and-daub houses. Beside them lay neat plots of corn, millet and barley that in just a few weeks would be ready to harvest. With the coming of the monsoon in June, the same plots would be flooded and turned into rice paddies. Some of the rice would be stored until the winter and sold to the Bhotia.

On the third morning, we sighted the graceful summit of Lamjung Himal, at the eastern end of the Annapurna range. Later in the day, we rounded a bend and glimpsed the massive bulk of Manaslu to the east. The two great peaks looked as remote as the moon.

Our motley caravan was headed by the Sherpas, who decided where to stop for lunch and for the night. The cook and the porters who carried the tents and the day's food accompanied them to have things ready when we arrived. The rest of us travelled at our own pace, and we were strung out over several miles, stopping often for refreshment at the many tea houses along the way. These open-fronted establishments sold alcohol—beer and a fiery spirit called *rakshi*—as well as tea, and a few porters would straggle into camp hours after the others, having spent most of the afternoon drinking.

Other travellers were on the road: villagers from Manang District walking down to the lowlands to buy or sell goods; muleteers from Lamjung District driving strings of plumed and belled animals laden with rice to Manang;

One of the largest and most ornate of Nar's many religious shrines (right) bears on its upper section a painted plaster face (above) whose tranquil gaze is a Buddhist symbol representing the Buddha's compassion for all living beings. Shrines are often erected beside mountain paths as well as in the villages, and the Bhotia usually murmur an invocation when they pass a shrine.

Hindu holy men with hot eyes returning from pilgrimage to Muktinath, a shrine in Mustang. This shrine, with miraculously burning stone, fiery earth and a flaming spring—phenomena produced by a seepage of natural gas— draws pilgrims from the great cities of India.

We climbed steadily throughout the fourth day. The next morning, we entered the narrow breach between the eastern end of the Annapurna range and the 26,000 foot summit of Manaslu. The hills closed in around us, confining the river to a deep gorge fed by waterfalls that seemed to descend in slow motion from hanging valleys filled with forests of fir and rhododendron. The river was a sickly grey-green colour and turbid with silt carried down from the cloud-draped Annapurna range. The steep path clung to the cliff face, occasionally crossing the river on sagging suspension bridges that swayed alarmingly in three planes at once. Ahead of me a porter lost his footing on the slippery track and was carried half way over the brink by the weight of his load. For a few seconds, grinning with terror, he hung with his legs dangling over the torrent before he managed to haul himself to safety.

My pocket altimeter registered 6,200 feet, and the evening air was sharp as we reached Thonje, the first village in Manang District. We entered beneath an arch surmounted by three cairn-like structures painted white and topped with yak horns. "Those are *chortens*," said Yonden, "Buddhist shrines."

The sight of the *chortens*—literally "supports for offerings"—told us that we had at last reached Buddhist territory: such structures are built as a pious act by Buddhists hoping thus to merit rebirth into a better existence and ultimately *nirvana*, a state of perfect harmony with the universe. Twenty-five centuries ago, the Buddha taught that life is an illusion and that life's desires lead only to suffering; salvation, he said, required the destruction of all cravings. Death was not the answer, because death was followed by rebirth into another form of life. The goal was to escape altogether from the weary circle of existence to *nirvana*. Buddhists strive towards that goal not only by compassionate behaviour towards every living thing but also by such special observances as building the shrines that we had passed, and that we were to see at the approach to every village, on every trail and at the top of many passes.

The Tibetans, among the most devoted and fervent upholders of the Buddhist faith, long ago intertwined the philosophical teaching of the Buddha with other strands to make a form of Buddhism that is peculiarly their own. Buddhism had already changed from its austere Indian beginnings before it first reached Tibet in the seventh century: the Buddha had become not merely a teacher but a god, and other deities borrowed from Hindu cults had joined him. Tibet contributed its own indigenous deities, potent forces residing in earth, air and water, which were incorporated into the Buddhist pantheon. In keeping with their previous characters, these Tibetan deities were portrayed in statues and paintings as terrifying demons—but with their fury now turned against the evil forces opposing the Buddhist doctrine.

The Tibetan form of Buddhism is distinguished not only by its followers' unshakeable devotion to the old local gods but also by its class of high priests, who are known as lamas. The Tibetans have a particular veneration for someone who teaches; "without lamas," goes one of their sayings, "there can be no approach to enlightenment".

We looked for the lama of Thonje but the village temple was deserted. Next day, however, we were more fortunate. On our way upriver again, Nik, Yonden and I stopped in a tea house to escape a downpour. Two men in traditional Bhotia dress were preparing to leave as we entered. They both wore Tibetan *chubas*—loose-fitting wool robes the colour of blood that hung to knee-length woollen boots patterned in red and black. Their long, black hair was braided into pigtails secured by red ribbons. Round each man's neck hung a bead rosary and a piece of raw, black-veined turquoise set between two discs of coral. An intricately stamped silver box bearing the portrait of a lama was tied to each man's girdle; Yonden explained that the boxes held amulets and talismans for protection against evil spirits and other dangers that might be encountered on a journey.

Yonden asked the strangers who they were, and one of them—who sported a wispy beard and moustache and had the features of a genial pirate—introduced himself. It was on this chance occasion that I first met Samten Phuntso, a lama from Nar who was to become a familiar figure to us during our stay in the village.

Speaking to Yonden in Tibetan, Samten Phuntso explained that he had spent the winter travelling round Gurung villages performing ceremonies, telling fortunes and selling herbal and magical cures. With the money he had earned, he had bought enough rice to tide his family over the lean period between winter's end and the next harvest. Now he and his companion were on their way back to Nar to prepare their fields for the spring planting. We tried to question the two men further but they were anxious to be on their way before night fell. They shouldered their packs of rice and left, walking with the slow, deliberate tread of mountain dwellers.

From this first encounter with Nar villagers, we discovered the language problems that awaited us. Samten Phuntso had spoken to Yonden in perfect Tibetan, but when he turned to his companion he had reverted to a dialect of Tibetan that Yonden could not understand, which we soon discovered was spoken only by the people of the Nar-Phu valley. Fortunately, almost everyone from Nar and Phu spoke Tibetan as well as their local dialects, and most spoke Nepali, too—but I was to find it frustrating that, every time I wanted to know what people were saying to each other, Yonden had to ask them to translate into Tibetan and then translate in turn to me.

Following in Samten Phuntso's footsteps, we reached the village of Kupar later that same day. This was as far as we would go along the Marsyandi; the Nar river spilled from its own small valley to the north into the larger stream at this point. Tired by six days of uphill walking with rain dogging our heels, we decided to rest at Kupar for two days before striking up the narrow Nar-Phu valley. On our third and last night at Kupar an avalanche swept down the terrible north-east wall of Annapurna II. All we heard was a faint grumble that gradually swelled to a roar and then died to an angry mutter. The air seemed to vibrate for a long time afterwards.

The next morning was the first clear one for days, and the mountains were ineffably beautiful. As we crossed the Marsyandi to enter the Nar-Phu valley, sunlight was creeping down the chiselled face of Annapurna II, illuminating plumes of wind-driven snow that danced along its crest and vanished like ghosts into the dark-blue sky.

We entered the valley through a gash barely a hundred yards wide that marked the end of the well-trodden trekking route and the beginning of the restricted border territory. The path was cushioned with pine needles and passed from pockets of shadow to pools of sunlight where magpies with iridescent blue backs and tails a foot long scolded us for our intrusion. Burdened with debris brought down from glaciers, the river rushed along its bed, gouging deeper into the earth. Working with all the time in the world, the water had grooved and hollowed the cliffs on each side of the valley, transforming huge boulders into sensuous sculptures. The walls of the valley rose almost vertically on either side of the river. Around noon we at last came to an open space and found that the advance party of Sherpas had already pitched our tents. Although they had never visited the valley before, they had learnt from natives of the region that we would find no other suitable camping place before nightfall.

We left the camp site early the next morning. In the sunless dawn, the deep valley was a cold and cheerless place. Above 9,000 feet, winter was giving way to spring with grudging slowness. Bamboo shoots were sprouting from earth that was still patched with snow, and buds of birch and willow spread a pale fuzz against the dark and spectral fir trees.

We traversed a dozen bridges during the morning, all built and kept in repair by the villagers of Nar. Where the river was narrow, it was bridged by a single span of logs lashed together. Wider stretches were crossed by cantilever bridges made up of two sets of tree trunks counterweighted on each bank by boulders. Wherever the track had collapsed, the gap was spanned by a simple bridge of birch trunks; where it met an unclimbable crag, a notched tree trunk served as a ladder. Although we met no one throughout our journey, it was evident that the trail was well-used: lengths of roughly hewn timber were stacked outside smoke-blackened caves; Buddhist invocations had been carved into the cliff face; scraps of cloth hung on trees to propitiate the gods and demons of the forest.

The river divided into two and the path continued up a steep hill that blocked the view ahead. At 11,000 feet, the pines and firs conceded defeat, leaving birches and junipers to straggle upwards. At 12,000 feet, I felt for the first time the effects of high altitude—breathlessness and a faint giddiness. Stopping every few minutes to drag air into my lungs, I painfully made my way up the last 1,000 feet and stood on the crest of the trail, gasping from the exertion—and at the view ahead.

On the eastern side of the valley, sunlit pastures mounted towards the 23,000-foot summit of Kang Guru, a massive sugar-icing dome flawed by shadowy crevasses and ice-falls. Yaks grazed on the hill; the chiming of the bells they wore drifted down to us. To the west, our maps told us that the village of Nar stood on a shoulder of pasture land that ran up from the river, but the village was still hidden behind Pisang Peak. Northwards, the valley narrowed again between mauve and ochre precipices veined with glittering quartzite. At the head of the valley, near the Tibetan border, an icy pinnacle rose in solitary splendour from a jumble of lesser mountains.

Below the hill where I stood, stone houses were scattered among terraced fields. This was Meta, the main winter settlement of Nar. Now, with the approach of spring, it was virtually deserted. A few yaks stood among the houses and some of the fields had been newly cultivated; but nobody appeared to greet us. A flock of snow pigeons burst from a crumbling three-storey house built like the keep of a medieval castle. It was one of three or four substantial buildings that suggested Meta had once been something more than a winter retreat. War or banditry may have compelled the inhabitants to move to a less vulnerable site; or, more likely, an avalanche or rock fall had diverted its water supply, reducing the area that could be cultivated.

Soon after Meta, the river and the path forked. One path went straight on, following the course of the main river up to the head of the valley and the village of Phu. The other path, to our left, would lead us to Nar, which we hoped to reach the next day; we would visit the smaller and more distant community of Phu at the end of our stay.

The trail descended again to the river, skirting a badly eroded hillside crowned by a ruined fort that commanded a bridge over a deep ravine. A

A notched-log ladder leading up from the courtyard to a doorway set high in the wall provides the main access to a Bhotia house (right). The upper storey is the family's living quarters; the lower floor is used to store grain and hay. Each house has a trapdoor in the roof, which may be closed with a wooden flap (above) and which, in some homes, serves as the main entrance.

herd of yaks on the other side of the river was racing in our direction, pouring through the junipers in a shining veil of dust. They came to the bridge and thundered across, then streamed up the narrow path towards us in a jostling, wild-eyed mass. Nik and I were forced to leap on to a large boulder while they made their way past. Grinning at our discomfiture, two boys wearing fur hats rushed after the yaks.

That night, still several hours' walk from Nar, we camped downstream from the bridge, between a deserted Buddhist temple and the largest shrine I had yet seen—a massive stone structure about 40 feet high, built in square tiers surmounted by a spired dome. As we were taking down our frost-rimed tents next morning, we saw a figure dressed in red approaching us through the junipers. He was a small, slight man with a thin face darkened by the sun. He introduced himself as Tsosang Sangma, a herdsman from the village of Nar who had been grazing his herd of yaks in a winter pasture farther downstream. One of his animals had fallen down a cliff and was mortally injured; did we want to buy the carcass?

We had not eaten fresh meat since we started out on our journey, and we readily agreed to go and look at the yak. Tsosang led us on a traverse of the almost perpendicular hillside, strolling with his hands clasped behind his back while we flailed and floundered in his wake on the loose-stoned surface. After about 20 minutes, we reached the edge of the side valley leading to Nar, and looked down to see the yak lying awkwardly in the stream-bed. As we climbed down towards the injured beast, it made an effort to stand upright, but only its front legs moved. A few feet away on the edge of the stream, a young yak grazed contentedly.

Three more people joined us as we inspected the yak—Tsosang's wife and his daughter and son-in-law. Like Tsosang, they were dressed in woollen *chubas* and homespun trousers that were tucked into the colourful Tibetan-style boots worn by all the Bhotia. The older woman had a strong-featured gypsy face framed in a sheepskin helmet. A black goatskin protected her back against the cold. The daughter had almond-shaped eyes set wide apart in a feline face. Over her sleeveless *chuba*, which was gathered at the waist with a broad, woven girdle, she wore a woollen apron woven in coloured stripes. The son-in-law was a thick-set, sullen-looking youth who stood a head taller than Tsosang. His black, unkempt hair was tied back in a pigtail, and he sported a pair of turquoise and coral ear-rings. With his swarthy, regular features, he could have passed as a Greek or an Italian.

After some bargaining over what we should pay for the yak, we finally agreed to buy the hindquarters, with the liver and heart thrown in free. But there was a problem. As a Buddhist, Tsosang could not take life, even to put an injured animal out of its misery. Yet the Bhotia are meat-eaters, a paradox made obvious by the presence in each village of a slaughterer—usually someone who is not a member of one of the established clans. There was a slaughterer in Nar, Tsosang explained, but unfortunately he was in the pastures with his yaks. It might take several hours before he could be found.

A crowd of villagers jostles for handfuls of
consecrated sand, scattered on the ground
during a rite to banish the evil spirits
held responsible for a chickenpox epidemic
that has killed several children in Nar.

bulging eyes, glaring black pupils and a mouth that gaped in manic rage. It was an effigy of one of the demons that, according to a diviner in the village, had caused the illness. Shaped from dough and painted a dark, ominous red, it would be a central figure in the remaining ritual. Beside it stood a large cone, also fashioned from dough, which would serve as a scapegoat towards which all the evil troubling the villagers would be directed. The two figures were pierced with cross-like structures whose ends were joined by coloured threads to form diamond shapes. By careful adherence to their ritual, the exorcists hoped to drive the demons into the spaces enclosed by the threads, where they would be trapped like flies caught in a spider's web, unable to inflict any more illness on the community.

As I watched, the old man I had seen the night before came into the temple. This was Nyendrak Singe, the head lama of the village, its religious leader and the man charged with protecting it from hostile spirits. The task that faced him now would demand all his skills in meditation and magic. To drive out the evil spirits the lama first had to enlist the help of a powerful guardian deity—a local god who, it was considered, had been successful in ridding the village of epidemics on past occasions.

To assist him in summoning the guardian deity, the head lama could call upon a number of lay brothers—Nar men over the age of 15 who could read well enough to recite their Buddhist texts. Chanting in teams of six, their role in the exorcism was to welcome the deity as an honoured guest to a feast. Thus they had arranged on the altar a selection of offerings: water for drinking, water for washing, flowers, incense, lamps, perfume and food. The first stages of the exorcism—the part I had seen the previous night and the ceremonies that I was now watching—were devoted to attracting the guardian deity's attention. Once they had invited the god to be seated and to partake of the offerings they would make their demands; only then would the struggle against the demons start in earnest.

On the third day the exorcism reached its climax. The guardian deity was now deemed suitably honoured. The number of lay brothers had risen to 14 and despite the gravity of the occasion, there was a sociable atmosphere in the temple. Wives brought meals to their husbands; a baby curled up on his father's lap, interfering with his cymbal-playing: small boys came to stare in awe down the mouths of the huge copper horns held by two youths, who chatted together as they waited for the cue to play. When the moment came, one player produced a splendid brassy note, while the other managed only a strangled bray. Unabashed by the reproving looks directed at him by the other participants, he grinned and exchanged instruments with his partner. With the new horn, he could produce no sound at all; and the two youths spent the next hour dismantling the instrument to locate the fault.

Suddenly, a man entered the temple wearing a brown, wide-sleeved gown; in one hand he carried a double-headed sceptre, representing a thunderbolt, and in the other a bell. He was just another of the lay brothers, but in this guise he symbolized the presence of the guardian deity. Taking up a position between the two lines of celebrants, the gowned figure advanced towards the altar with a kind of swimming motion. The music swelled and, with a crash of drums and cymbals, he lunged at the cone of dough, brandishing his thunderbolt and his bell. He stopped short of touching the figure and then retreated down the nave.

For an hour the dancer advanced and retreated, advanced and retreated, miming the battle that was taking place with the evil spirits. Seven other villagers, also dressed in long gowns, entered the temple and joined in the dance. Five wore broad-brimmed hats; the others snatched down from the temple's central pillars masks bearing the warlike features of village deities. Once more the main dancer made his stately advance on the effigies, but this time he did not retreat. He lay down the sceptre and bell and, triumphantly lifting the figures over his head, gyrated wildly, then carried them down the nave and placed them by the door.

An expectant crowd of villagers had assembled in the courtyard outside the temple. Two of the dancers picked up the dough figures and headed a procession up the hillside to a flat piece of ground near our camp. There, the effigies were set down and the villagers formed a circle enclosing them. A lama walked round the assembly, carrying a basket filled with sand that had been consecrated by being kept in the temple during the ceremony. He scattered handfuls of sand over the villagers to remove any lingering contagion. When the purification had finished, people fought for the remaining sand and carried it home with them to help expurgate any traces of the evil spirits.

Only the dancers remained, their robes flapping like giant crows' wings as they whirled. Light was draining fast from the sky, and in the gloom straw was piled under the demon-figure and set alight; the cone-figure was left for the ravens and choughs. Still dancing, the masked and black-hatted men made their way back down the hillside and disappeared into the darkness.

The ceremony was over. For the moment, the villagers were safe, but none of them imagined their victory was final. The evil spirits had been banished, not destroyed; in one form or another, they would be back.

Villages Linked by Tenuous Trails

The villages of Nar and Phu lie concealed in one of the most inaccessible valleys of the Himalayas—an enclosed region that is virtually unknown except to the villagers themselves.

Among the screes, cliffs and dizzying gorges of the branching 20-mile valley, travel is possible only by steep and precarious paths, and constant maintenance is required to keep them open. Landslides and avalanches may sweep away whole sections of the trail without any warning. The most vulnerable bridges are dismantled at the beginning of each summer to save the precious wood from being carried away by the rising rivers,

The main track out of Nar (background, centre) rounds a bluff above the cleft of the river, before winding eastwards to join the route that leads up the

forcing travellers to take higher and more difficult routes. Although some of the trails are wide enough for bulkily laden pack animals, many are so narrow, steep and tortuous that they admit only human traffic, walking and climbing in single file, and unladen animals.

Distance in this majestically rugged terrain is measured in walking days, not in miles; an uphill journey may take a whole day longer than the same route downhill. The path between Nar and Phu, which is shown on the following pages, covers less than 15 miles on the map, but for a laden traveller the trip means a laborious and often harrowing two-day trek.

larger arm of the valley to Phu. Only one other path leads west from Nar out of the valley, over a high pass blocked by snow from December to March.

Climbing back up the path with loads of firewood gathered further down the valley, a party of Nar villagers files past the ancient shrines and prayer

wall that mark the outer limits of the village. Travellers always show respect for such buildings by keeping them on their right hand as they walk by.

Glimpsed from the track as it skirts a steep
slope outside Nar, a temple (foreground, left)
and an ornate shrine occupy a patch of level
ground beneath a towering wall of jumbled
rock. The buildings are maintained by
the inhabitants of Nar as a religious duty.

A wooden bridge carries the path across
the river's yawning chasm to a vertiginous
promontory. Up-river to the right lies
the way to Phu; the higher of the two
paths to the left of the bridge leads to Nar.

A line of yaks unhesitatingly crosses the flimsy-looking but meticulously kept bridge that is guarded at each end by a shrine in the form of a gateway.

Toiling up the path towards the village of
Phu, four heavily laden travellers negotiate
a twisting rock-hewn stairway and a
sagging bridge of wood and stone that has
been constructed to span an awkward gap.

In a narrow defile where the river has sliced a deep channel, hundreds of neatly piled stones form a ramp leading up to a high, slanting shoulder of rock.

Crossing a steep scree slope, the path loops round a small shrine so that all travellers may keep it on their right as they pass.

Prayer flags shredded by the wind and stones inscribed with prayers consecrate an ancient gateway built near the head of the valley to mark the entry into the territory that immediately surrounds Phu village.

Once threatened by bandits from Tibet, the village of Phu huddles like a fortress above sheer walls of rock 100 feet high. The approach to the village

winds past terraced fields—the only touch of green in the arid valley—round the foot of the cliffs (foreground, left) and up the narrow gully beyond.

Two | **A Threefold Livelihood**

The struggle to rid the community of demons and disease had preoccupied everyone in the village. But with the crisis over, the villagers could concentrate on the no less pressing business of making a living. Each season is dominated by one of the three occupations—trading, herding and farming—that together provide their livelihood. Winter is the main trading season; spring and autumn are concerned with sowing and harvesting crops; in the summer months many Bhotia leave Nar with their flocks of sheep and goats and their herds of yaks, moving by stages to higher and higher pastures to exploit all available grassland. Now, in late April, it was time for the spring planting—one of the busiest periods of the year for the people of Nar. For the next month, every family's prime concern would be to work its fields.

Most of the villagers had got back to Nar only within the last few weeks. They had left the Nar-Phu valley with their livestock in early January, before Nar was cut off by snow and its pastures buried under drifts up to 10 feet deep. Some had spent the winter tending the animals at the settlements of Meta and Chaku, below the tree line. Both places offer a limited amount of grazing, which is supplemented by fodder—grass that has been cut earlier in the year and hung in trees to dry in the sun out of the reach of animals. Other villagers had migrated south to the lowlands to trade. Only a few old and infirm people who could not walk had remained behind in Nar, together with a handful of able-bodied villagers who were paid to keep the flat rooftops clear of snow. But with the coming of spring, families were united again, ready to embark on a new agricultural year.

To get ready for the ploughing of the fields, the yak herds had to be brought back from the pastures. Three days before planting was due to start,

Yonden and I accompanied Tsosang Sangma on an expedition to round up his yaks. Some of the strongest beasts would be tethered in the small yard below his house and used for ploughing; the others, he said, would be grazed in a small pasture across the river from Nar until the time came to drive the whole herd to their summer pastures.

We left the village soon after daybreak. The morning air was fresh and light, but the sky was dull in the east—a sign of impending bad weather. Since our arrival, winter had been fighting a rearguard action against the slow advance of spring. Although the sun at mid-morning was hot enough to burn our skin, at midday clouds usually began to spill over the peaks from the east, arriving over the village with a rush of wind and a patter of stinging hail that later turned to snow.

The weather was taking its toll of the village livestock. In the past few weeks the lower mountain slopes had become smudged with green, but the new grass was pale and too sparse for grazing. The sheep and goats had nothing to eat except last year's shrivelled growth. The cattle were suffering even more. Most of the families keep one or two cows to supply them with milk in winter when the yaks are dry; unable to extract enough nourishment from the valley's withered shrubs, the beasts are kept in the village and fed on stored hay until the new grass comes through. But many households had exhausted their stocks of fodder and could only watch helplessly while their cows starved. Four had already died, one of them with an unborn calf.

Only the carrion-eaters benefited from these hardships—for them, it was a time of plenty. A pair of ravens had taken up residence above the village. Cold-eyed scavengers with pick-axe beaks and baggy pantaloons, they would descend each day to strut with a proprietorial air among scraps of rubbish in the streets; and as I followed Yonden and Tsosang along the path leading east out of Nar, I could see them loitering with malicious intent near a group of new-born lambs. They were always first at a carcass.

We walked towards the glistening mass of Kang Guru mountain, following a whale-backed ridge bounded by the Nar river to the south and the Thepche river to the north. Red-and-black chats flitted ahead of us, alighting on thorn bushes to deliver an alarm call that sounded like pebbles being knocked together. The turf was springy underfoot, but in places the ground had been cropped bald by sheep and goats, allowing wind, water and frost to scour out the earth and expose bare rock. Cries rang in the brittle air as boys and girls chivvied their flocks; the young shepherds carried baskets to collect dung for the hearth fires. A mile from Nar, we stepped over the rough stone wall that marked the limit of the Nar home pasture. The turf within the boundary, Tsosang explained, was grazed mainly by sheep, goats and cattle; the yaks grazed more distant pastures.

As we walked along the ridge, Tsosang pointed out the main grazing areas belonging to Nar. West of Nar were two large summer pastures. The main winter pastures were concentrated in the Nar-Phu valley, around Meta and Chaku. Farther to the east, beyond the snowy range running south from Kang Guru, a high mountain pass descended into a sheltered valley called Namya, two days' walk away and unmarked on any map. Tsosang told me that Namya had a less arid climate than Nar; it therefore supported more vegetation and could be grazed all year round. There were drawbacks, though. Wolves and snow leopards lived there, so Tsosang said, and the valley was sometimes so misty that yaks could be located only by their bells. Herdsmen who use Namya's pasturage in winter stay in caves or crude stone houses, cut off until March by the snow-blocked pass. To share out the grazing, the villagers alternate pastures annually: those who winter in Namya one year take their herds to graze around Meta and Chaku the next, and vice versa. Tsosang himself had overwintered this year in an isolated house between the two settlements, by the side of the Nar river, and it was in that direction that we were now heading. After the ploughing, he told us, he would be taking his yaks to one of the two large summer pastures west of Nar.

Later, I calculated that Nar's grazing lands were scattered over a territory of about 200 square miles. Most of this area is a desert of snow fields, precipices and scree slopes, but it includes sufficient pasturage to support a population of about 2,000 yaks. At the time of our visit, the most prosperous family owned more than 100, but some householders had as few as five. For convenience, many combined their animals with those of their relatives to make larger herds that were tended either by the owners and their families in rotation, or by hired herdsmen whose wages were paid collectively by the owners. For grazing purposes, there were 24 yak herds, divided into two groups of 12 that were kept apart except at the height of summer.

The grazing always followed a regular routine. The arrangement this year would begin with one group grazing the mysterious valley of Namya, while

the other grazed the land west of Nar and in winter the pastures around the lower settlements. In June, the Nar herds would be driven to Namya and all the yaks would graze together for a month, leaving the Nar pastures empty. Then all the herds would be driven back to Nar for a month, their arrival marking the beginning of the *Dardzi*, a midsummer festival celebrated with dancing, archery contests, horse-riding and much beer-drinking. In August, the herds would again be divided into two groups. Those that had spent most of the year around Nar would be driven to Namya, while the 12 herds that had been in Namya took their turn at grazing the Nar pastures. The purpose of these complicated manoeuvres is first to prevent overgrazing, by leaving each main area of pasture empty for a month at the peak of the growing season, and secondly to ensure that each yak owner gets his fair share of the best—and worst—pasture land.

Beyond the home pasture, the Thepche river had taken a great bite out of the ridge, which dropped down to groves of straggling birches. We stood on the edge of a 1,000-foot precipice, inhaling the warm, scented air that rose towards us from the pines and junipers far below in the Nar-Phu valley. Three

A winter settlement of crude stone houses lies enclosed by mountains in a bowl of land hundreds of feet below the permanent villages of Nar and Phu. Their lower altitude gives such settlements a milder climate, providing refuge for Nar and Phu families and their livestock during the coldest months. Now, in late spring, most of the houses are deserted and only a few sheep and goats remain to graze the pastures.

griffon vultures flew out from their nesting colony in the river gorge below, and gained height with slow flaps of their eight-foot wings. They sailed over the valley, drifting like sunlit motes of dust above the shadowy depths; then they found an updraft, set their wings and turned in the direction of Nar, passing overhead in line-astern formation and coming so close that I could hear the wind sighing through their stiff primaries. Like the ravens, the griffon vultures are attendants on death: twice in the last week I had surprised a squabbling group of them with their long, bald necks buried deep in the soft parts of a calf's carcass.

After about an hour's walk, we caught sight of Tsosang's herd scattered in a mile-long arc along the ridge. The first four yaks we came across were cropping in a hollow on the edge of the slope; another four started nervously when we emerged from behind a rock outcrop; 10 more, driven by a youth, were climbing slowly up through the birches; the rest of the herd of 72 were filing towards us along the main path to Nar, with a second young herdsman in their wake. With staccato cries—*ca ca ca ca ca*—and a few well-aimed stones, Tsosang began to round up the small groups and drive them towards the main body of the herd. I walked beside him, admiring his beasts and listening to him extol their virtues.

Tsosang's yaks supplied him with food, milk, fuel, cloth and shelter; with goods to trade and a means of transport; and with the muscle power to pull his plough. They were, in short, his most valued possession, combining the virtues of draught oxen, dairy cattle, packhorses and sheep. Tsosang took an obvious pride in his yaks, and indeed they were highly attractive animals, with noble heads, sad, liquid eyes and glossy, wavy coats of black, white, beige, honey, chocolate, smoke grey and combinations of these colours. Long, silken hairs hung like a curtain from their flanks, making their short legs look even shorter. Behind, they sported plume-like tails in which every hair seemed to have been individually oiled and combed. Most had horns, symmetrically curved and armed with viciously sharp tips.

Each of Tsosang's yaks had its own name, which described its colour or, more rarely, its temperament. He boasted he had no difficulty recognizing his own animals, even at a distance. Waludong was a beige-and-grey animal flecked with white; Nadi was black with a white patch on its head; Lakjok was a fast, nimble animal with a fiery temperament; Shachen was a dull beast that was always wandering away from the herd. While scanning the gorge below us with powerful binoculars, I spotted two yaks on a piece of pasture outside a cave on the other side of the Thepche river. I assumed that they were strays from Tsosang's herd, but he squinted at the distant specks and confidently pronounced that they belonged to another herdsman who had already driven his herds to a high pasture for the summer. The cave, he added, was a winter refuge for three families and all their sheep, goats and cattle; their yaks were left in the open to graze the surrounding area. The two strays had wandered back to their winter pasture.

As we returned to Nar with the herd, Tsosang described the ways in which his yaks provided for his household. Mindful of the Buddhist prohibition on

Hunched against a bitter blast of May sleet, a young boy who has been hoeing the fields blows on one hand to try and warm it and hides the other deep within the folds of his voluminous robe. The occasional showers of snow and sleet that still fall at this time of year can destroy the newly planted seeds.

taking life, he was reluctant to admit how many of his animals were slaughtered for food. No doubt one or two were killed each autumn and their meat smoked for the winter; but during our stay in Nar, the only meat I saw the villagers eat was scraps of dried yak meat chewed as a snack. Nevertheless, yaks are a valuable source of nourishment: their blood, tapped from their veins with a knife when they are fat on new grass in summer, is heated with *tsampa* and the mixture shaped into cakes to be stored for the winter. From May to October, the female yaks give milk which is turned into curds, whey, yogurt, cheese and, above all, butter. Yak butter, blended with tea and eaten with *tsampa*, forms the staple diet of every family. The butter has many other uses. It is moulded with dough into votive cakes for the gods; kneaded into hides to make them waterproof and pliable; rubbed on the face and hair as a cosmetic and screen against the sun and desiccating wind; and clarified to provide the oil for lighting and altar lamps. Yak dung is used as fuel for the cooking fires and manure for the fields.

The thick wool of the yak is woven into blankets, tent cloth and ropes. The shearing of the animals takes place in midsummer, when the villagers have returned to Nar for the *Dardzi* festival. Most of the animal's coat is sheared with a knife, but a different method is employed to remove the long, silky belly-hairs that are woven into tent cloth. The tents are used in the highest grazing pastures, where there is no other kind of shelter from the weather for the herdsmen. To make the material waterproof, Tsosang explained, the belly-hairs have to be pulled out by the roots, since cut ends, apparently, make a less water-resistant cloth. The process sounded a painful one. The yak's hind legs are tied together so it can be thrown to the ground and immobilized, then the hairs fringing its belly are wrapped around a stick a couple of times and yanked out.

As pack animals and mounts, yaks can function at altitudes of up to 20,000 feet, puffing like steam-engines in the thin air. Strong, solid and sure-footed, a yak will travel all day at a plodding pace of two to three miles an hour, and is able to maintain its speed uphill by bunching the great hump of muscles on its back and thrusting itself forward with head lowered. It can also move at a delicate, high-stepping trot. Yaks can jump nimbly down a six-foot drop, negotiate a mountain track that is only inches wide and keep their balance as they wade through torrents of water that would sweep away a horse. Snow is their natural element—they can plough through chest-high drifts with ease, clearing a path for men to follow.

The domesticated yak's incredible stamina and adaptation to high altitudes is inherited from its wild ancestor—a massive animal that still inhabits the bleakest parts of the Tibetan plateau. Among the Tibetans, these beasts have acquired a reputation for vindictive cunning that strains credibility. According to Yonden, a team of three men was needed to hunt one. Each hunter would dig himself a small hole in which to lie in wait until a yak came within shooting range. Once it had been shot, Yonden informed me, the mortally wounded yak would use its dying strength to revenge itself on the hunter by collapsing over his hole, imprisoning him by its sheer bulk. Only

Two pairs of boots, temporarily discarded by their owners who prefer to work a muddy field barefooted, lie beside a pot containing the worker's midday meal of rice. The boots, worn by Bhotia men and women alike, are made by stitching woven wool uppers to supple leather soles cut from yak hides.

The rice balls and beer would later be redistributed among the villagers, with extra shares going to the lamas as a payment for their services.

What had begun as a religious occasion turned into a social event, for instead of resuming their work, the villagers sat in groups chatting. In one corner of the field, a woman suckled her baby surrounded by friends, who were discussing the planting, and children who played around their mothers' legs. In another corner, a group of men was holding an animated discussion over a piece of paper, as they tried to work out where the nomad shepherd should take their flocks when he returned from Meta. After about an hour, the villagers dispersed, taking with them their juniper sprigs. Like the pagans of pre-Christian Europe, the Bhotia credit the sweet-smelling juniper with the power to avert evil, and the sprigs would be planted in the middle of their own fields to protect their crops.

Next morning, the shouts of herdsmen floated across the valley as the yaks chosen for ploughing were driven down from the nearby pasture and into the village. Tsosang, though, was enjoying a leisurely breakfast of rice with his family; unlike most people in Nar, he had sufficient dried fodder left to keep his plough team tethered in the village. From my vantage point outside his house, I could see more than a hundred yaks milling across the Nar river and stampeding through the fields, drawing shouts of protest from the owners of the neatly raked plots. The herdsmen trotted behind their recalcitrant animals, alternately soothing and cursing the beasts and occasionally stopping to respond to the teasing cries of encouragement and abuse that came from the women gathered on the rooftops.

A beautiful white yak rushed past me rolling its eyes, hotly pursued by an excited boy of about eight who was swinging a yak-hair lasso. Panting along behind them came the owner of the yak, a man of advancing years who also rolled his eyes at me as he passed. Another man headed off the yak and forced it to turn in the direction of its pursuers. It made a dash between them, but the boy deftly tossed the coiled rope over its horns and hung on gallantly as he was dragged across the field. The men went to the boy's assistance, hauling on the rope until the yak was on a short tether. Dodging an angry thrust from the animal, the boy succeeded in grabbing it by its horns, giving the men time to hobble it and throw it to the ground. A wooden ring was passed through the yak's pierced nose, a rope was passed through the ring, and the now-subdued beast was led to the village where a well-earned breakfast awaited the men.

When he had finished his own breakfast, Tsosang shouldered a light wooden plough and led three of his yaks to the fields, leaving the other three munching fodder in the yard of his house; their turn at ploughing would come the next day. Tsosang's wife and daughter, his son-in-law and a hired hand followed him, the daughter carrying a sack of barley seed. Tsosang had 40 fields in Nar—small, rectangular plots totalling about 20 acres. Like most of the other villagers, he also owned a couple of fields at one of the winter settlements, where he grew buckwheat. Because Meta and Chaku are situated at a lower altitude and have a milder climate than Nar, the fields there are planted and harvested about a month earlier. One or two members of each family stay on at their winter settlement until early April, to cultivate their fields and graze their livestock on the new spring grass before they return to Nar to help prepare for the main planting.

A few of Tsosang's Nar fields were grouped together, but the rest were widely scattered; because fields change hands regularly through inheritance and as part of marriage settlements, nobody has all their fields concentrated in one area. That day, Tsosang intended to plant 10 of his fields to the east of the village. Water from the irrigation channels had already begun to soak into the soil. Nar's water supply is insufficient to irrigate the entire cultivated area at the same time, so the channels carrying water to the eastern fields would be blocked off at the end of the day, and the water diverted to other holdings around Nar.

At the first of his fields, Tsosang harnessed two yaks to the plough, leaving the third to chew hay until one of the team tired. Meanwhile his wife and daughter filled woven grass baskets with manure from a pile protected by a juniper branch and scattered it over the earth. The fertilizer was a mixture of straw, cow dung and human excrement; the villagers often use the edge of the roof, above the cow pen, as their lavatory. When the manure had been spread, Tsosang's son-in-law filled a small basket with barley seed and scattered it thinly on the soil. All but three of Tsosang's fields would be sown with barley, two would be planted with potatoes and the last would be given over to mustard, grown for the edible oil that is pressed from its seeds. Curiously, it was only after the sowing that ploughing began. There was barely a foot of soil above the solid mountain rock, and the purpose of ploughing was to cover the seeds, not to prepare the ground for them.

Before he started ploughing, Tsosang gathered his family around him and placed a dab of butter on their heads. Then he anointed the yaks in the same way, and placed another smear of butter on the tip of each horn. Muttering the *Om mani padme hum* formula, he guided the plough while his son-in-law led the team, and the other helpers used rakes to turn over the earth in the corners of the field where the plough could not reach. When the whole field had been ploughed, the women lightly raked over the surface of the soil, then finished by piling up a ridge around the field to prevent the irrigation water from draining away too quickly.

The same scenes were being repeated in most of the fields to the east of Nar, an area more than half a mile square. Flocks of choughs flew overhead like scraps of charred paper, chirruping and whistling companionably as they descended to feast on seeds and insects. Eddies of snow pigeons joined them, settling for only a minute before rising again in a swirl of white wings. The valley was a pattern of colour and movement—the mosaic of eccentrically shaped fields, with the newly ploughed earth standing out from the unturned soil; the black and white birds in their shifting formations; and the red-coated men and women, shrunk by distance, moving back and forth, back and forth, to the age-old rhythm of the plough.

Tsosang finished planting his fields within four days; his son-in-law, said the other villagers with a trace of envy, was one of the hardest-working men in the village. However, in such bleak conditions no amount of industry is proof against disaster: at any time during the growing season, snow and frost may attack the crops. Only a week after Tsosang had planted his first barley, heavy snow did indeed bring work in the fields to a standstill. At five o'clock one morning, I awoke from a dream in which an avalanche had swept down Pisang Peak to find two grinning Sherpas beating snow from my tent, which sagged within a few inches of my nose. Cursing, I went back to sleep; and when I woke again a few hours later, the world was white. Three inches of snow had fallen during the night, and flurries continued to fall until the afternoon. The villagers spent the day clearing the snow from their rooftops.

That afternoon, when Samten Phuntso walked up to our camp, I asked him what effect the abrupt change in the weather would have on the village. The snow would make planting impossible for two days, he said. Some of the seed already sown would have rotted, so that many families would have to resow fields they had planted—if they had any seed left. I asked if the crops were ever totally destroyed. "The harvest is not gathered until October and November," he replied. "Snow begins to fall a month before that. Sometimes half the crops are lost." Samten Phuntso's philosophical acceptance of these hardships inflicted by the weather was shared by everyone in Nar. Each household was well aware that until the harvest had been safely gathered

In the yard of a Nar house, yaks wait to be
divested of their wooden pack saddles after
transporting bundles of firewood collected
from the edge of the tree line, several hours'
steep walk down the Nar-Phu valley.

into their store in November, it would be reckless to even calculate the yield. The only thing they knew for certain was that it would never be enough.

Tsosang's household exemplified the economic facts of life at the uppermost margins of habitation. Provided that his herds were not struck by disaster, his family was self-sufficient in dairy products. In fact, there was often a surplus of butter and cheese. But arable land was so scarce round Nar that even in a good year his fields provided only enough cereals to last his family for nine months. And Tsosang was well-off compared to many villagers. The head lama, for example, owned the same number of fields; but because he was too old to work them himself, he had to employ field hands and pay them a proportion of the harvest. They received two-thirds of his crops, leaving only enough grain to feed his household for about four months. Rich or poor, no one in Nar could subsist by farming and herding alone. It is trade that gives the Bhotia of Nar a critical edge over their environment.

From midsummer through autumn, they raise cash by selling yaks and yak products to the Manangbas, the people who live in the Manang village area and who provide a guaranteed market for Nar's livestock. Occasionally, the buyers come to Nar, walking or riding on horseback over the mountains at the height of summer; but usually the Nar villagers journey to Manang. In July, Tsosang told me, he would drive three to five of his yaks to Manang and sell them to his trading partners—four men whom he had known and dealt with for many years. The buyers would fatten the yaks on their lusher pastures for two months and then butcher them to sell at a profit in their villages. He had an arrangement with the buyers whereby he retained the hides and tails. He kept the hides to make the moccasin-style boots that all the villagers wore, but sold the tails in Kathmandu, where they were bought by Hindus who used them as fly whisks and ceremonial objects. Later in the year, Tsosang would load one or two yaks with butter, dried cheese and a few homespun blankets. In Manang, he would trade the butter and cheese for wheat and buckwheat, and sell the blankets for cash.

Each family in Nar had similar arrangements, usually long-established. Trading partnerships with the Manangbas are passed down from father to son on both sides; the Manangbas depend on yak products from the Nar villagers because they have largely abandoned herding. Like the people of the Nar-Phu valley, the inhabitants of Manang, Pisang and the other villages in the valley north of the Annapurna range are Bhotia; and until the 18th century, they too were primarily pastoralists and cultivators. But in the 1780s—according to local inhabitants—they were granted special trading privileges by the ruler of Lamjung, in return for taking his side in a war against another local potentate. With licences to import and export goods at favourable rates of duty, they were encouraged to develop trade at the expense of herding and farming. They still grow crops, but the men are frequently away on trading expeditions, and their fields are worked almost entirely by women and hired immigrants from Tibet.

Traditionally, the Manangbas dealt in yak tails and blankets, leopard skins and musk, which they sold in India and Burma. But by the time we visited

Weighed down by a load of clay pots that she bought in the village of Chame, one day's walk down the valley from Nar, an elderly woman pauses on her way home to check her purse. She makes two or three such short trading trips each year, selling herbs or juniper incense and using the cash to buy extra food and household utensils.

Nar and Phu, they had branched out into manufactured goods and had extended their trading ventures to cover most of South-East Asia.

Lacking the trading privileges of the Manangbas, the people of Nar have never engaged in such far-flung ventures. Even now, all their trading is done in Nepal. During their winter sojourns in the market towns of Lamjung District, in Kathmandu and in villages *en route* to the lowlands, they raise the cash to buy grain and other essential commodities. In addition to yak wool and tails, blankets and dried cheese, they sell medicines and incense made from herbs and juniper, which they gather in the pastures during summer. Lamas can earn a few rupees by telling fortunes, treating illnesses or exorcising evil spirits in the Gurung villages of Lamjung, where such services are in great demand: the Gurung villagers have a saying that the only true lama is a lama from Nar. Nar people who do not have such specialized skills to offer hire out their labour. Hearing of a caravan of rice being taken north up the Marsyandi the men will join up as porters, leaving their wives and sisters in Manang to do a few days' work planting wheat in the fields of absent farmers. Few people stay in one place for the whole winter. In one village, a family may sell some incense and use the proceeds to buy chilli; the next day they will move on to another village and sell the chilli at a profit. With the cash raised from each transaction, the family can buy a little more grain to take back to Nar; and for their daily needs, they feel no qualms about begging. When they begin the slow trek home in spring, each person is laden with goods—even six-year-old children carry their own packs of rice.

Thus Bhotia children are introduced early to the demands of necessity: the same necessity that has taught the Bhotia their trading skills. At first sight, it is curious that a people living so far from any commercial centre should have developed such entrepreneurial flair. But the amount of food each Nar family will have to live on until the next harvest depends in large measure on the success of their winter trading ventures, and the fact that few households go hungry is testimony to their enterprise.

A Backbreaking Term in the Fields

For two weeks every spring, the fields surrounding the village of Nar hum with strenuous activity as the villagers till the soil and plant the few crops—mainly barley, but also potatoes, radishes and mustard—that can prosper in the bleak climate, high altitude and rugged terrain. The rush to get the planting completed is dictated by the weather. If the seeds were sown before late April, frosts would kill them; but if planting were delayed beyond mid-May, the crops would be ruined by the onset of winter before they were ready to harvest.

Preparation for planting the seeds begins in early April, as soon as the villagers return from the lower altitude settlements and trading places where they spend the winter. The whole community combines forces to repair the walls that separate the terraced fields and to clear the irrigation channels that transport water from the Nar river. When the communal labour is completed, each family sets to work to till its own collection of small, irregular plots, which in most cases are scattered throughout the village's cultivated area of about 1,000 acres. Since the ground is too hard and dry for the lightweight ploughs to furrow, an advance task force of women breaks up the brittle clods with mattocks and spreads manure over the thin topsoil. The seeds are broadcast, and only then do the men follow with their ploughs to turn the manure into the soil and bury the seeds. For the ploughing, each family relies on the strongest of its yaks, which during the brief period of planting are left to graze close to the village; each morning, the chosen beasts are rounded up and harnessed into teams of two to draw the ploughs.

After the ploughing, the yaks are released from their stoical servitude and driven to the summer pastures. Their masters, too, enjoy a period of respite from the fields: while they tend the yaks, the women weed and irrigate the growing crops. But autumn brings a second intensive bout of labour for everyone. First comes the harvesting of the potatoes, radishes and mustard. Then the barley is cut with sickles and stacked in the fields in sheaves. The villagers carry the sheaves on their backs into Nar where they thresh the grain and spread it on their rooftops to dry before storing it in their houses. An average yield lasts a family about six months, and must be supplemented by buying rice from the lowlands during winter.

Leading two yaks and carrying ploughs and rakes, a group of villagers negotiates a path atop one of the low stone walls dividing the terraced fields.

Ankle deep in freshly turned earth, a woman (centre) bends low as she swings her mattock to crack the dry, caked surface of a field bordering the Nar river. Her fellow workers have paused to pull out potatoes left in the ground after the previous year's harvest.

Hurling a yak-hair lasso at the head of a wary beast, a boy conducts an early morning round-up of some of the yaks needed for the day's ploughing.

Draped across the edge of a terrace, a young man slumbers beside his spade after a long and exhausting day spent working one of his family's fields.

Three | **Family Cross-Currents**

During the last few weeks of the planting season, Nar had been largely deserted as the villagers laboured in their fields, never stopping work except to snatch meals in the open, and returning home only when it got too dark for them to guide the ploughs. We alone had time on our hands, and we spent it going from rooftop to rooftop, gratefully pouncing on anyone with a moment's leisure to talk to us. It had been a frustrating period: although I had found out plenty about herding and farming, my knowledge of family life and village organization was still slight. But in the lull that always follows the planting, as the villagers returned to their household chores and prepared for the move to the high pastures, I at last had an opportunity to learn about the ties that bind families and neighbours together into a community.

Usually, the way a people gains its living influences the way it orders its society. What makes the Bhotia of special interest is that they combine three livelihoods, each of which tends to promote different social values. On the one hand, their mobile herding life encourages individualism. Spending weeks at a time away from their villages, the Bhotia must be self-reliant and free of obligations to people outside the immediate family. Their trading activities likewise foster independence and, to some extent, egalitarianism; for among people who live by trade, status is often measured by wealth, and even a poor man can improve his social standing simply by making a successful business transaction. But their third occupation, farming, tends to produce a much more interdependent society. Since agricultural resources are limited, one cultivator can only increase his prosperity at the expense of other members of the community.

To find out how these different strands were woven into the fabric of Nar society, I decided to take a closer look at a typical family—which in Nar comprises all those relatives sharing a household. Although the villagers cooperate as a community when it is in all their interests to do so—for instance,

herdsmen do not graze their animals wherever they wish, but follow a pre-scribed pattern of rotation—they live together for only about three months of each year, mainly during planting and harvesting. For the remainder of the year, individual families go their own way. During the six months spent in the high pastures, and in winter when they disperse on trading ventures in the lowlands, the members of a household rely on one another almost totally.

Charlotte suggested that I talk to Komi Tsering, whose family she had got to know well. Komi duly arrived at our camp one morning and invited us to his house. He was not an imposing figure. Dressed in a frayed and much-patched *chuba* that he wore with the upper part tied around his waist as a concession to the heat of the day, he was a slightly built man in his fifties, with unruly hair and intelligent, rather simian eyes. He was married, with four daughters, one of whom had a baby boy; he was also the chief member of one of Nar's four clans. Though by no means well off by Nar standards—he owned only 30 yaks, he told me, and his fields were among the most un-productive in the valley—he was obviously a man of some consequence in the village, for as we walked through the narrow lanes on the way to his house, he was greeted with respect by everyone he met. Later, however, I was to discover that Komi's family had a skeleton in its cupboard, one known about by everyone in Nar except us.

Some of the villagers who addressed Komi were old women complaining of chest pains, or mothers with feverish children. Several men in Nar prac-tise herbal medicine, but Komi, it seemed, was something of a specialist in the traditional Tibetan art of blood-letting, and though I never discovered whether his bleeding treatments worked, he did not appear to lack patients.

We arrived at Komi's house and climbed the ladder to the roof, where his wife sat crooning to their one-year-old grandson as she tenderly rubbed his plump body with butter to prevent the skin from chafing. A few rooftops away, an ancient-looking woman was giving herself the same soothing treatment. Gleaming with butter, the baby was dressed by his grandmother in a miniature *chuba* and laid on a blanket in the sunshine. Komi, usually an undemonstrative man, began playing with the child, teasing him with a stick until his wife sharply told him to stop and get on with some work.

The Bhotia consider it wrong to hit a child or address it angrily, and their children are obviously indulged. In Nar, even the 76-year-old head lama—a man of impressive solemnity at most times—allowed his two grandchildren to clamber over him and pull his beard while he recited his morning prayers.

The people of Nar have cause to regard their children as precious, for they have only a frail hold on life. At least half never reach their fifth birthday, and one woman told me that only four of her 12 children had survived infancy. Children are rarely left unattended during their first few years of life. Wrapped in a sling or, more commonly, cradled in a wicker basket, they accompany their mothers or older sisters to the springs, fields and pastures.

From an early age, however, Nar children are expected to help with the work of the household. Carrying is mainly women's work, and it is common to see girls of seven or eight staggering along under a water pot or a basket of dried dung, spinning wool as they go. Indeed, spinning is an automatic activity for both sexes and all ages—something to occupy the hands while walking along or talking with neighbours. Both boys and girls spend whole days looking after their families' sheep and goats in the home pasture. For the boys, this is but the first step in learning to control animals; from the age of about 10, they begin accompanying their fathers and older brothers to the yak pastures, and by the time they are 12 or 13, they are expected to be adept at herding, lassoing, saddling, loading and driving yaks. Girls of the same age spend much of their time in the village—roasting and grinding barley for *tsampa*, making beer, weeding the fields and weaving. But they, too, are frequently away from home—sometimes in the high pastures helping to milk the yaks and make butter and cheese, sometimes in the winter settlements herding sheep and goats, tending the fields or collecting firewood. It is rare for all the members of a household to be in the village at the same time.

Of Komi's four daughters, for example, the eldest, Sham Drolma, was training to be a nun at Braga Gompa, the largest and most important temple in Manang District. His second daughter, Pemba, and her 25-year-old sister, the mother of the baby, were away that morning gathering juniper branches to make fences round the newly planted fields, while the girl's husband, Komi told me, was visiting his parents. The youngest girl, 18-year-old Yangdzom Tsering, was staying in Chaku with Komi's teenaged nephew, tending the family's sheep and goats.

In many societies, conventional morality would be outraged at the idea of teenage boys and girls being left alone together overnight. In Nar, however, where work goes on simultaneously in the village, high pastures and winter settlements, it is an economic necessity. Not surprisingly, children have their first sexual experiences at an early age, and many boys and girls are no longer virgins by the age of 16. As an old woman told me: "When the young

as he entered the village he slipped away to a friend's house, where he stayed throughout the betrothal ceremony.

When the families had exchanged greetings, they retired to the bride's house to toast the alliance with the beer provided by the groom's family. The groom's two brothers presented each of Nyima's relatives with a *kata*—a white scarf that is always given by the Bhotia on important social and religious occasions. Nyima herself stayed in the background, helping to serve her guests with beer and food. Speeches followed, some traditional and some more impromptu, fuelled by the freely flowing alcohol. The details of the marriage settlement were recounted and then, with Nyima and her absent groom now formally engaged, the floor was cleared and the husband's family formed a semicircle and began to dance. More beer flowed, Nyima's relatives were drawn into the line of shuffling dancers, and the groom finally joined the gathering. The dancing in Nyima's house soon broke up, but the party continued in her relatives' homes. Long after midnight, groups of guests were going from house to house, leaving behind those who had succumbed to sleep or drink. Next morning, the bleary-eyed hosts bade farewell to their hungover guests as they left on the journey back to Nar.

It was not until 10 years after they had been betrothed that Nyima set up house with her husband. Riding on horseback, she was escorted to her new home by her brothers and an uncle. After beer had been drunk and the dowry handed over, she was left to begin her married life in Nar.

I found it difficult to believe that as long as 10 years could elapse between the formal betrothal and the wedding ceremony after which the couple actually began living together. But the other women I spoke to confirmed that a long delay—more usually between one and four years—is customary.

There are several reasons why engaged couples, even after they have had children, wait so long to set up home together. One is personal preference: it is considered hard for a girl to have to leave her parental home, and all the women I talked to criticized marriage on the grounds that it uprooted them from their own families. More important is the economic factor. In Nar, as in other Bhotia communities, most households consist of only parents and their unmarried children living together as a largely self-sufficient social and economic unit. When a married couple begins living together, the husband's parents are expected to provide them with their own home; and since it costs the equivalent of 10 to 12 yaks to build a house in Nar, parents tend to delay the break-up of the family until they are willing and able to meet the cost of the couple's home—perhaps when the father becomes too old to manage all his animals and fields and is happy to turn over some of his property to his son. Until then, the couple work exclusively for their respective parental households. Once they have set up their own home, however, they are under no obligation to work for anyone else—although relatives do, in fact, combine their labour for demanding tasks such as ploughing and herding.

For the betrothed couple, enforced separation is not as irksome as it might seem. The woman frequently visits her fiancé, staying at his parents' house

Ignoring a heavy snowfall, a villager rinses his hands outside the main temple after eating rice balls to celebrate the communal effort of repairing the irrigation channels; the boy facing him polishes off the last grains in the dish. In the temple annexe there is a kitchen area, where festive meals and the food offerings for rituals are prepared.

and sharing his bed; the couple are therefore free to enjoy each other's company while being spared the responsibility of managing their own livelihood. Any children conceived during this time are cared for during their first years in the relative prosperity of the grandparents' home. By the time a couple sets up house together, they will usually have a child old enough to help work in the fields and pastures.

In some Nar households, there is a different arrangement: the young married couple lives permanently with one or other set of parents. Tsosang, for example, had no sons, so when his only daughter married, he invited the husband to move in as a resident son-in-law, with rights of inheritance to some of the household property. This arrangement—standard practice in a family without sons—provides the household with an extra worker while retaining the services of the daughter. If Tsosang had had several sons, he would have arranged it differently: the elder sons would have set up separate households when they married, but the youngest would have stayed on in the parental home, which would pass to him on the death of his parents.

Laws of property and inheritance help to explain the most unusual form of marriage among the Bhotia: polyandry, where one wife has two husbands. Since sons inherit equal shares of the parental wealth, there is a likelihood that none of the heirs will receive a portion of the property large enough to support a separate household. To avoid this, two brothers may agree to marry the same woman and pool their resources. The villagers told me that polyandry had never been a Nar custom, although it was common among the Sherpas, in Mustang and in Tibet.

Polyandrous marriages do not always work. Often, the younger brother tires of the older woman and will want a younger one for his wife; or the brothers fall out when one accuses the other of not contributing enough to the household. However, monogamous marriages in Nar are not very stable either. Sexual infidelity is not regarded as a serious breach of morality and the villagers have many opportunities to indulge in casual affairs when their marriage partners are away trading or herding. Because most of the marriages are arranged economic alliances rather than love matches, dissatisfied partners may break off the relationship when they find a lover of their own choosing. A number of villagers I spoke to had divorced their first partners and embarked on second marriages.

When couples split up—either during the separation following the *Rikchang* ceremony or after they have started living together—they do so without any formal ceremony. If the wife has run off with another man, the lover is obliged to compensate the jilted husband with property equal to half the value of the marriage settlement. If the husband dissolves the alliance, the wife keeps half of the marriage gifts. In fact, so many marriages end before the couple actually begin living together that a wife is not allowed to dispose of any part of her settlement before setting up home with her husband.

I asked Nyima who managed the affairs of her household. "We both do," she replied. "Our money is kept in a chest, and if either of us needs any, we take it. When one of us wants to buy something expensive, we discuss it first.

We discuss everything." From the first, I had been impressed by the forth-rightness and self-confidence of Nar women. What Nyima said confirmed what Christoph had found among the Sherpas and other Bhotia communities: wives take an active part in the decisions affecting the running of the household. While husbands make most of the decisions concerning yaks, the buying and selling of animals and the timing of seasonal movements between pastures, wives manage the fields and house, and have an important say in what proportion of dairy products shall be traded.

While I was talking to the women, I noticed a villager going from rooftop to rooftop, collecting *tsampa* and yak butter from each household. Nyima explained that he was a member of the village council, who was collecting offerings for a community ritual.

There are various groups responsible for regulating community affairs in Nar. Three men act as guardians of the fields, ensuring that water for irrigation is properly distributed and that landowners do not encroach on their neighbours' fields. Another group of six men sets the price of certain commodities, including beer, fodder, timber, salt and eggs. It surprised me that such staunch *laissez-faire* capitalists should allow price-fixing—but I was told it was necessary to prevent individuals from establishing a monopoly and charging other villagers whatever they liked. Even Nar's religious activities are organized by two men whose duty it is to ensure that lay members attend the rituals, and that temple discipline is maintained. They have

Absorbed in their own tasks, two villagers work companionably on a rooftop while the granddaughter of one plays quietly beside them. The man on the left is mending a yak-hair rope affixed to the wooden saddle in front of him. His turbaned neighbour spins wool on a simple hand spindle of the sort commonly used by both men and women.

the authority to impose fines on offenders—people who fail to pay their temple dues, for example, or who turn up drunk at a ceremony.

The most interesting civic group is the *gampa lendzin*—the village council, which organizes major festivals and rituals, manages the pastures and forests, and collects taxes. The council consists of seven members—three *lendzin*, who investigate complaints brought to them by the other villagers, and four *gampa*, who act as judges. Like the other groups who help run the village, the council is open to all male householders. Members are not elected, but appointed in strict rotation for one-year terms.

The duties of the council are not particularly onerous, and membership carries undeniable advantages; besides providing a public service, the *gampa lendzin* is a profit-making organization—with the profits going to the serving members. At the beginning of each year, the outgoing council hands over a budgeted fund of 1,100 rupees to the new members. From this sum, the *gampa lendzin* is obliged to pay a land revenue of 330 rupees to the Manang District Office in Chame, and to donate a small living to the three senior lamas. The balance is the council's to use as it wishes for the personal profit of the members—provided that it passes on the sum of 1,100 rupees at the end of its year in office. Generally, the council uses the money to buy rice, which it then sells at a profit to the other villagers; or it may contribute some of the money towards purchasing a yak, which it sells to the Manangbas.

The *gampa lendzin* has various other sources of income. It owns several fields, worked by villagers who are paid with part of the harvest. The rest of

A young child snugly wrapped in a double layer of blankets peers from the security of a wicker basket carried on his mother's back. Strapped behind him is a prayer book with carved wooden covers whose pages contain invocations designed to protect the child from any malevolent spirits.

the harvest is sold in the village, and if council members want some of the yield themselves, they have to pay for it like everyone else. The council also has exclusive rights to an area of winter pasture that is never grazed, but cut each autumn for fodder that is sold to the villagers. Disputes over grazing rights fall within the *gampa lendzin's* preserve. It is the council that co-ordinates the seasonal moves of the yak herds in Nar, and it has the power to fine a herdsman who grazes his animals on the home pasture out of season, or whose animals stray and destroy crops.

The council also raises revenue from the forests below Nar. The bulk of the income from this source comes from Phu, which has no trees in its own territory. When Phu villagers want timber for building, they are obliged to buy it from Nar at a cost of three rupees per tree. Nar villagers are exempt from this charge, but they are only allowed to fell timber in certain areas stipulated by the council. Breaches of this rule are punishable by a fine, as is cutting living trees for firewood. Either the villagers were extraordinarily law-abiding or the council rarely invoked its authority, because Tsosang told me that nobody had been fined for such offences for five years—a record that, I regret to say, was broken by our porters, who returned to camp one day with loads of green wood. I paid the fine.

Every household in Nar pays the *gampa lendzin* taxes on land and ani-mals—half a rupee for each yak, a smaller sum for each sheep and goat, and five rupees for each unit of farming land, which the Bhotia measure by the amount of grain needed to sow it. On top of these dues, herdsmen must give the council about two pounds of butter for every 12 female yaks they own.

Near the end of the council's term of office, it is traditional for the mem-bers to organize a ritual hunt, apparently to celebrate the legend of the found-ing of Nar, when a hunter discovered the valley after following a blue sheep he had wounded. Each autumn, five or six men are selected to hunt blue sheep in Lhemoche, a high pasture north-west of the village. They leave after being feasted on rice and beer and sometimes stay in the mountains for sev-eral days. On returning, according to custom, the hunters hand over to the *gampa lendzin* the carcasses of any sheep they have killed, but keep the horns and skins. Then the council members and the hunters celebrate with a party at which they feast on the blue sheep.

Before leaving office, the *gampa lendzin* holds a party exclusively for themselves, at which they balance the books and share out the profit they have made. It is unlikely that any council member enriches himself unfairly during his period of office; the possibilities for defrauding the other villagers are minimal. Nor does the office lend itself to abuse; any member tempted to settle a grudge by unfairly fining someone would be discouraged by the fact that next year or the year after, his victim would be on the council. All in all, the *gampa lendzin* seems a very democratic institution.

Until more recent years, the *gampa lendzin* had much greater powers. The members judged both marriage and property disputes and—except in the very rare cases when a murder or other serious crime was committed—criminal offences. Nar was virtually autonomous. But in 1976, as part of a country-wide reform, the Nepalese authorities established an administrative centre in Chame, with a District Officer empowered to hear and judge disputes brought to him by villagers under his jurisdiction. In addition, the District Officer acted as a channel for aid to the outlying villages. The traditional village councils were superseded to a large extent by councils called *panchayats*—elected bodies that reported to the District Officer.

In Nar, the *panchayat* consists of 11 members—nine ordinary members, a woman who represents women's interests, and a member who is responsible for liaising with the similar *panchayat* in Phu. It is difficult to say how much the *panchayat* system has affected Nar. Some changes have occurred as a result of requests for aid. The village now receives funds for bridge-building and maintenance of tracks. It has a government-paid postman—a villager who goes to pick up mail in a cave half-way between Nar and Chame. It even has a school staffed by three Hindu teachers who teach the rudiments of Nepali reading and writing to a handful of pupils. But centuries of independence must have made the villagers wary of taking their disputes to outsiders, and I got the impression that most of them prefer to settle their internal affairs amongst themselves. Disputes with Phu are another matter, however.

Since the *panchayat* system was introduced, I learnt, two disputes had flared up between the two villages. The first concerned a piece of pasture that both villages claimed as theirs; the District Officer settled it by decreeing that Nar and Phu should graze the pasture in alternate years. The second dispute was not so easily resolved. Aggrieved at having to buy timber from Nar, which controlled more forest than it needed, the Phu *panchayat* complained to the District Officer, who ruled that the Phu villagers had the right to fell timber near Chaku, Nar's most northerly winter settlement. But Nar paid no heed to the judgement, and when a party of Phu woodcutters tried to claim their right, they were turned back by a band of Nar men. As a result, relations between the villagers had so deteriorated by the time we arrived that Phu had broken off marriage negotiations between Nar and Phu families.

The only dispute I came across in Nar involved Komi Tsering and one of his clansmen. Komi was leader of the Erphobe clan, to which 14 of Nar's 61 households belonged. Membership of a clan is hereditary and although it does not confer any political power or recognized social status, each clan takes pride in its own history, and the longest-established in a village tends to think of itself as socially superior.

The duties of a clan leader are mainly ritual ones, such as making daily offerings at the clan temple and performing blessings on clan members. Clan heads have no formal civic standing, but occasionally they will be asked to mediate on behalf of clan members involved in arguments over property, marriage and other issues. Komi himself was frequently called on for advice and help, less because of his position as head of the Erphobe than on account of his reputation for being "a man of *dharma*"—a devout and conscientious person. Charlotte and I visited him one morning to find him engaged in conversation with several men, one of whom seemed highly agitated. When I asked what the discussion was about, he told me that the villager was his

On the rooftop of a neighbour who has one of the half-dozen stone handmills in Nar, a woman grinds Tibetan rock salt and chats to the mill's owner.

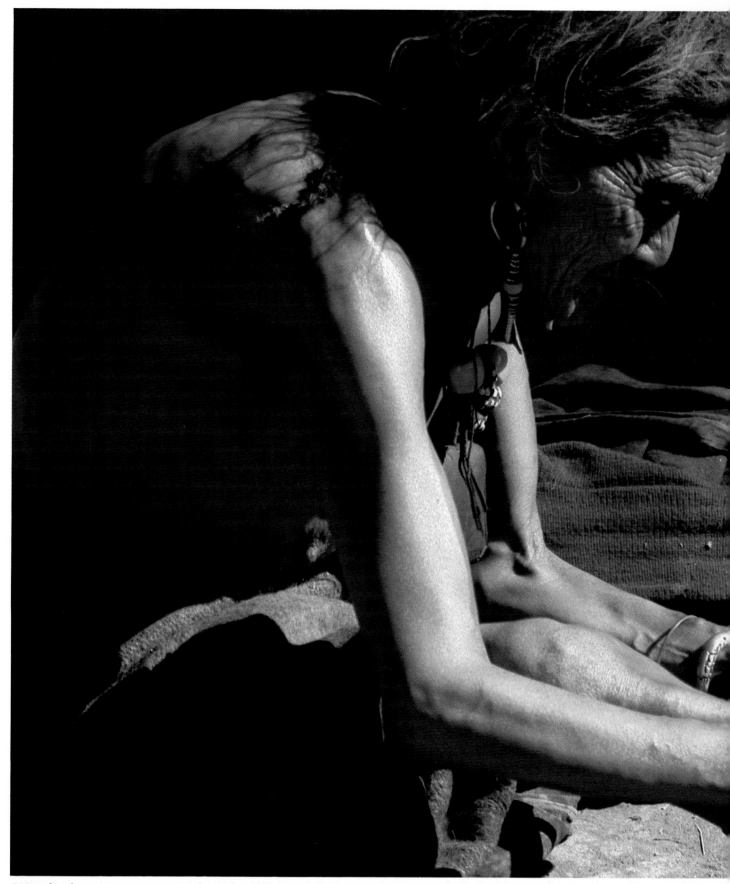

Stripped to the waist, a woman anoints her body with butter-oil. Both men and women use clarified yak butter to lubricate their cold-chapped skin.

to say, the Sherpa who had so selflessly aided his friend gained so much merit by this one act that he, too, obtained a good rebirth.

During another visit, the head lama described some more conventional ways in which a Bhotia fearful of judgement day could add to his store of merit. Prayers, either said privately or commissioned from a lama, would bring merit; so would planting prayer flags, building a *chorten* or donating money to a temple—"although if you worship with money and not with your mind," he insisted, "you will gain nothing."

Pilgrimages are a popular means of acquiring virtue, since they satisfy the Bhotia love of travel and can be combined with a trading venture. Most of the Nar men had visited the holy shrines and sites in Kathmandu, while the head lama had taken part in an epic six-month pilgrimage to Mount Kailash, a sacred mountain in western Tibet. Soaring 22,000 feet in symmetrical splendour, the peak is the inspiration for the mythical mountain that stands at the centre of the Tibetan universe. But sadly, the lama never reached the fabulous mountain. "The Chinese invaded Tibet during my journey, and I had to turn back," he told us regretfully.

Just as he had explained the paths of virtue to me, so the head lama would give informal instruction to any villager who came to ask advice about a problem. He also held more formal courses for villagers who wanted to take part in temple ceremonies. Each autumn, any man over the age of 15 could spend a short period of retreat in the main village temple, where the head lama taught how to make offerings and prepare an altar, how to perform the rituals that would bring long life, health and other material blessings, and most important of all, how to read and recite the sacred Tibetan texts. Those who had followed the courses called themselves *Chopa*, "men of religion"— a position similar to that of a lay brother in a Christian community.

There were also a few nuns in Nar—shaven-headed girls who did not marry and who, like Komi Tsering's daughter, went away to Braga Gompa for their religious training. The nuns often performed private ceremonies for families, but never, to my knowledge, took part in temple rituals, although they did join in the recitations for major rites held outside the main temple.

Nyendrak Singe had other duties besides teaching. As a diviner and astrologer, he could read the portents that told of danger threatened by demons; as a master of ritual, he led the ceremonies to placate deities and, if necessary, to expel evil forces. He was also a healer, with a wide range of cures to remedy the afflictions of villagers. And his concern for their welfare went even beyond life: one of his most important roles was that of guide to the spirits of the newly dead.

Everyone in Nar agreed that the head lama's powers in these matters were unsurpassed. But certain other villagers had similar strengths themselves, and, with Nyendrak Singe's advancing years, they were increasingly called on to exercise them. Two senior lamas—both of them men who had studied religion for many years under his guidance—helped him perform village rituals; one of these was Samten Phuntso, my first acquaintance from Nar. The leaders of the village clans presided over their own ceremonies in separate

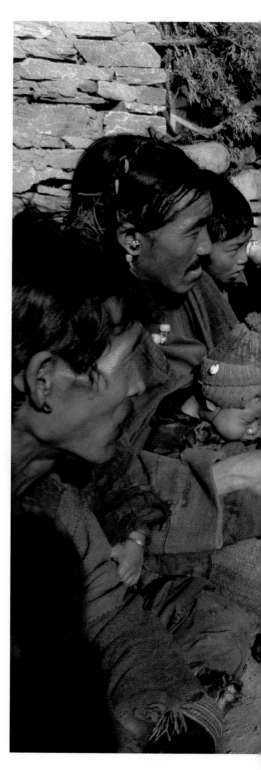

Before an attentive crowd, a lama casts a
villager's horoscope by consulting a text and
two complicated astrological charts that
are spread, one on top of the other, on the
ground in front of his low wooden table.

clan temples. A number of villagers had medical and herbal skills; and many more claimed some insight into the future—for in Bhotia society, almost everyone is a soothsayer, and omens are read in everything from the cry of a bird to the shadows cast by a fire.

The desire to see into the future is universal: how many people in the West turn eagerly to the horoscope columns in their morning newspapers? But among the Bhotia, divination is an essential part of decision-making—an attempt to satisfy a need for certainty in a capricious world. There are no weather forecasts to help the Bhotia decide when to plant their crops; no road reports to tell them if a trail is passable; no stock market bulletins to tell them the current price of salt; no newspapers or radio to inform them of conditions beyond their own valley. Yet because of the inimical climate of the Himalayas, and because their enterprising spirit takes them on long trading expeditions and pilgrimages through hazardous and unknown territory, they have a pressing need for information. To find out the risks involved in any venture, to forestall calamity, or simply to decide on a course of action, the Bhotia consult a diviner.

In enlisting the help of a diviner, a man will be sustained by the firm belief that no misfortune can occur accidentally. For the Bhotia, every event is a link in the chain of cause and effect, so that by projecting perception forwards into time and space, calamities can be foreseen and steps taken to avoid them. Whereas the majority of Westerners live perpetually on the border between past and future, Buddhist philosophy holds that time and space, like all earthly phenomena, are mere projections of the mind, which can be trained through meditation to see beyond the immediate present. The head lama of Nar was reputed to have such meditative powers.

Most diviners, however, do not claim to be time travellers, and although several other villagers were respected forecasters, astrologers or diagnosticians, they used mechanical devices to obtain their results. The simplest of these devices requires no divining skill, but can be used by anyone needing to make a choice between alternatives. One such device is the bead rosary that every Bhotia wears. If a traveller on an unfamiliar path comes to a fork and is not sure which direction to take, he may select an arbitrary length of his rosary and divide the beads by a random number; depending on whether the result is an odd or even number, he will take the right or left fork. When a more detailed answer is required, the diviner may throw a dice, having assigned each number a different meaning, or place seeds on a drum and read the patterns that appear as the drum is beaten. Freaks of nature are seen as omens: when we were in Nar, a ring around the sun was interpreted as a sign that an important person would die. Strangely enough, we later learnt that the head lama of Manang had died two days after the ring appeared.

For a more complete look at what the future holds in store, the Bhotia refer to a diviner-astrologer, who will prepare a full horoscope. Returning to our camp site one day, I found some of the Sherpas sitting in a circle round Samten Phuntso, listening with absorption as he told Yonden's fortune. Spread

In his role as doctor, a lama (right) feels the pulse of a woman who has come to him with an ailment. Once he has diagnosed her problem, he weighs out on scales (above) his prescription—lumps of reddish crystalline rock that he instructs her to grind up and take with milk. Several Nepalese coins in the left-hand dish serve as counterweights.

Passing a wall with a row of metal prayer wheels embossed with invocations, a villager reaches out automatically to revolve each of them in turn.

Slabs covered with prayers lie on a hilltop beside a shrine. A few villagers carve their own prayer stones but commissioning one also brings merit.

prayers for her recovery. Yonden carried out the head lama's instructions and Lhamo's condition improved considerably.

The strange thing is that something did happen to Lhamo at the bridge on our journey to Nar. She had travelled ahead of us, and after crossing the bridge had looked back to see us inching across a treacherous, scree-filled gully on the other side of the gorge. When we joined her, we found her in a state of near-hysteria: seconds after we crossed the gully, she claimed, three boulders had hurtled down it and crashed into the gorge, almost taking us with them. Nobody else had seen the rocks fall; and neither Lhamo, Yonden or any other member of our party had told Nyendrak Singe of the incident. But how he found out about Lhamo's frightening experience is not important; by displaying an apparently supernatural knowledge of the matter, he increased her faith in the treatment prescribed.

The head lama had recommended prayers and offerings as a remedy for Lhamo's condition because he believed that spirits were the agents of her illness. But in other cases, he frequently applied his extensive knowledge of herbal medicines as an additional or alternative treatment. He told me that he used more than 30 different varieties of plant, most of them collected in the high pastures. The few that I saw were all distinguished by an unusual appearance. The most efficacious, used to treat everything from bronchitis to blood-poisoning, was called "summer grass, winter insect", and looked remarkably like a caterpillar with a blade of grass growing from it. Another, a root, was shaped like a tiny hand; not surprisingly, it was used to treat hand ailments, among other illnesses. The reputation of these herbal medicines goes beyond Nar, and many villagers raise cash by selling them during their winter migrations to the lowlands.

While Nyendrak Singe was regarded as a specialist in all areas of medicine, several other villagers in Nar were also respected doctors. There was Komi Tsering who, as I had seen, was often called upon to perform bleeding treatments, using a small knife and a needle that he kept in a little scabbard tied to his girdle. His other prescriptions tended to vary according to what he thought of the patient. To one old woman, he sold a medicine made from red crystalline rock; to another, he gave no prescription but answered sharply that her illness was caused by her neglect of her house gods. But his advice in the case of children who were weak and feverish from the chickenpox epidemic seemed straightforward and sensible: a light, mild diet consisting of barley porridge, milk and water, with no chili, meat or beer.

In spite of various medicines prescribed, and the head lama's attempt to exorcize the evil spirits responsible, the chickenpox epidemic continued to take its toll. Early one morning, Tsosang arrived at our camp to tell us that the disease had claimed another victim—a 10-year-old girl—during the night. Her funeral would be held that day.

Immediately after the death, the girl's relatives had summoned Lama Samten Phuntso to extract the spirit from her body. The Bhotia believe that when a person dies, the spirit that resides in the body and survives death will try to cling to what it knows rather than going out to meet its destiny in rebirth. For this reason, a Bhotia funeral is not an act of remembrance, but a rite of passage from one life to another. The lama who conducts the ceremony acts as the spirit's guide to its next existence. After commanding the girl's spirit to leave the body and renounce its attachment to its past life, Samten Phuntso plucked a few hairs from the crown of the corpse's head to encourage the spirit to pass out. Then one of the relatives took a piece of the girl's clothing and, speaking to no one lest the spirit attach itself to them, induced it to follow him to the head lama, who performed a rite to give him control over the spirit. Meanwhile, Samten Phuntso consulted his astrological chart to determine who could touch the corpse, how it should be disposed of, and when.

By now, most of the villagers had gathered on their rooftops to watch the funeral preparations that were taking place on the roof of the bereaved family's house. Nine lay brothers and four nuns were reciting prayers while the head lama and the two lamas next in seniority sat drinking tea and eating *tsampa*. Female friends and relatives of the family were busy preparing large pots of rice and *tsampa* for the wake that would follow the funeral; some would be offered to the spirit of the corpse to assist it on its passage.

The dead girl's mother and elder sister emerged from the house, weeping inconsolably and chanting a refrain. Stunned and withdrawn, the girl's 14-year-old brother sat apart on a corner of the roof. When the lamas had finished their food, they went down to the room where the body lay. The corpse, covered with a cloth, had been placed in a foetal position, symbolic of birth, in a corner of the room occupied by the family altar. Above it hung a painting of the Wheel of Life, showing the six spheres of existence clutched in the hands and feet of the Lord of Death. Sacrificial cakes and bowls of water had been placed by the body, together with more than 100 butter lamps.

The lamas and their lay assistants sat down in two rows facing each other and, after a blast on a conch shell, began their chanting. The text for the occasion was the *Bardo thodrol*, known in the West as the Tibetan Book of the Dead. While the chanting continued, the dead girl's mother and sister went round the room lighting the butter lamps, singing all the time the same keening refrain I had heard on the rooftop:

>We loved you, but now you are dead.
>You have left us. Go to your lama.
>He will show you the way.

Oppressed by the heat from the butter lamps, the crush of people and the profound grief of the dead girl's mother, I left the room.

Three hours later, unseen by any of us, the corpse was borne away to the Nar river. Lama Samten Phuntso had divined that the girl should be buried in the river bed downstream from the village, so that her disease should not contaminate the community. By the time I found out where to go and arrived at the spot, the burial was over.

Burials are in fact comparatively rare among the Bhotia. So concerned are they that the spirit of a dead person may linger on in the body—or even enter the body of someone living—that they usually destroy corpses. In Nar, only

A row of villagers, seated cross-legged in
front of planks piled with ritual books, jugs
and dishes, ring hand bells during a rooftop
ceremony aimed at bringing to an end a
siege of sickness raging through the village.

the bodies of children under eight are buried as a matter of course. Most other corpses are either burnt or, more commonly, dismembered and fed to the vultures—a grisly spectacle I witnessed when, shortly after the 10-year-old girl's funeral, an old woman died.

The body was kept in the woman's house for three days while the last rites were carried out; the period between death and disposal of the corpse can be as much as four days if the lamas believe that the spirit is loath to quit its body. Early on the third day, the funeral party left the house, led by 10 of the villagers blowing bone trumpets and beating small hand drums. Behind them came one of the senior lamas, holding a 10-foot length of blue-and-white ribbon. The ribbon was attached to the corpse, which was carried in a woven basket on the back of a villager. The dead woman had been placed in a sitting position and was shrouded in a length of green material. In the rear of the funeral procession came the dead woman's relatives and friends, weeping and wailing. Just ahead of them were two men carrying an axe and a *kukri*, the traditional curved knife of Nepal.

The procession walked through the village and down to the river, where the women stopped, forbidden to go further, but continued their plaintive chanting. The men walked on a little way until they reached a circle of flat ground amid large boulders. Arranging themselves in a group a short distance from the circle, the 10 leaders of the party sat down and began chanting, while the man carrying the body set down his burden in the centre of the circle. A ritual intonation began, occasionally punctuated by trumpet blasts.

"They are calling the vultures," Yonden explained. "If the woman has lived a good life, they will come soon; but if she was sinful, they will not come for a long time. They are praying to the king of the vultures. When he comes, the others will follow. If the vultures do not come, the corpse will be buried."

Half an hour passed. The two men who had been carrying the weapons stood up and examined their blades critically, then began sharpening them on rocks. In some Bhotia villages, the men who dispose of bodies are people of low status, but in Nar and Phu the task is performed on a rota basis. The man with the axe was the dead woman's son-in-law. When the two men were satisfied that the axe and knife blades were sharp enough, they walked to the corpse and, without any ceremony, tipped the naked body on to the ground. They arranged it so that its eyes were staring blindly upwards. The man with the *kukri* cut off the woman's ears, which were still decorated with turquoise ornaments; her clothes and jewellery would later be shared out between the ritual butchers and the corpse-bearer. With a single stroke of his *kukri*, the man cut off the corpse's head.

Working with stoic indifference, the two men cut off the woman's arms and legs, opened up the stomach, and proceeded to hack the entire body into small pieces. They did not simply leave the pieces where they fell, but picked them up and placed or draped them on and over the surrounding rocks. The butchery continued for about an hour.

Unconcerned by the gory scene being enacted only yards from where they sat, the villagers went on with their chanting. When they had finished, they

A woman's corpse, in a container draped with dark cloth, stands on a rocky knoll. In the background, villagers bang drums and chant to call birds of prey to the scene. The funeral rite ends with the body being hacked to pieces for the birds to devour.

moved to a spot a little to one side of the circle. The two butchers joined them, and all the men sat down and waited.

The choughs came first. Chattering and whistling like a witches' coven, they descended in dozens, attracted not so much by the pieces of flesh as by the scraps of sacrificial cake that lay abandoned where the chanters had sat. An hour passed. High in the sky to the east, a speck appeared. Slowly, drifting on angular wings eight feet in span, a lammergeier approached. It passed overhead, turned and glided low over the circle, its strange red basilisk eyes clearly framed by the black "beard" that bristled below its golden head. The lammergeier not only feeds on flesh, but also picks up bones and drops them from a height in order to break them and get at the marrow. Several times when I had been climbing on the mountain slopes around Nar, I had sensed something behind me and turned to see a lammergeier lazily soaring within a few feet—giving credence to the tales of travellers who have claimed that lammergeiers actually try to dislodge them from awkward slopes by brushing against them with their huge wings.

But the lammergeier was not the king of the vultures. After making several sweeps over the remains of the corpse, it gained height again and took its stand on a crag overlooking the valley. Two more lammergeiers appeared. They, too, did not descend, but found perches on the surrounding cliffs.

Morning gave way to afternoon. It looked as though the vultures would not come. But suddenly one of the men pointed excitedly skywards. Three griffon vultures sailed over the rim of the surrounding cliffs, and as they approached, more massive, square-winged silhouettes converged over our heads. Then an extraordinary thing happened. One of the vultures detached itself from the rest and descended. It did not glide to earth, nor did it dive; it seemed to fold its wings round the air and drop slowly down like a parachute—right into the circle of death.

The vulture surveyed the scene with pale, unblinking eyes, then unhurriedly hopped to a piece of flesh. The air sighed, and another vulture landed; the rest kept station overhead. A raven joined the vultures at the feast. Above the circle, choughs wheeled and swooped.

When the funeral party was satisfied that the fowls of the air had brought the death rites to an end, they left. The griffons, sated now, sat stupidly on rocks, so laden with food that they could not fly. High on the crags, the lammergeiers waited for the bones.

A Pageant to Expel Evil

Every May, the people of Nar mark the end of planting with one of their major festivals, a local version of a rite traditionally held throughout the Tibetan world. A three-day event involving much prayer-chanting, it is intended to safeguard the community in the coming months by diverting evil forces into effigies made of dough. When the figures have absorbed the forces, dancers bear them through the village, then fling them—and, symbolically, any harm they harbour—to the four points of the compass.

The ceremony is directed by Nar's head lama, who conducts both the initial rites in the temple and the ensuing procession with an air of

On the last morning of the three-day festival, the head lama sits tranquil and reflective on his carved seat in the temple. To help him during the ritual,

quiet authority. But the most conspicuous participants in the procession are the dozen-odd villagers who are given the honour of carrying the effigies—men dressed in black hats and sweeping robes who whirl through the winding streets invoking the power of the Buddhist faith to protect the community. Another group of villagers smear their limbs with ash and don masks to represent various heavenly beings, and join the black-hatted men in their exuberant dance. The rest of the village crowds round the dancers, watching every step and joyfully anticipating the climax that will cleanse Nar of evil for another season.

the lama can call upon more than 40 villagers, each of whom has had sufficient training to be able to follow the religious texts used on this occasion.

flesh with his knife, he had the skin off in 15 minutes. As he cut, he intoned *Om mani padme hum* to help the animal to a better rebirth. He stretched out the skin to dry; he would use the soft pelt to line a winter *chuba*. He kept the meat to make a stew, but since the goat had not been healthy, he threw the liver, heart and intestines to the waiting crows. He rinsed the blood from his hands with buttermilk; then, using an abrasive mixture of earth and dried goat's droppings, he scoured the buttermilk bowl.

Another Kyang resident dropped by, and for the next couple of hours the two old men sat in the sunshine by the side of Tashi's house, sharing a dish of curds and chatting. The brief exchanges about their families and flocks were broken by long, amiable silences. When his friend got up to go, Tashi went back to the roof and picked up another goatskin he had spread out to dry the day before. He sat cross-legged, silently mouthing a prayer as he kneaded the skin to soften it.

The afternoon slowly unwound. Dorje and Kamsum were still out of sight; Pemba was absorbed in a game of

He starts to skin a kid that has just died.

An old friend pays a leisurely visit to share a bowl of curds and a desultory chat in the afternoon sun.

A flat rock is worth humping home for structural repairs.

hopscotch under a juniper tree, her young flock temporarily forgotten. Griffon vultures turned in the great disc of sky above Kyang, while a lammergeier sailed overhead, circled on raked wings and then dropped down to snatch up a bone.

Tashi registered its passing with a flicker of his eyelids. In spite of the measured, repetitive rhythm of his days, he was never bored: the concept of boredom did not exist for him. As a young man, he had travelled far from the valley. He had been three times to Kathmandu, making the pilgrimage to the great Buddhist shrine at nearby Bodhnath. Bodhnath had awed him, and undoubtedly his pious journeys had earned him merit. But Kathmandu itself, with its teeming lanes and packed markets, he had found bewildering.

Twice Tashi had gone to Tibet's great northern plain to bring back salt, travelling in constant fear of bandits and enduring dust storms and blizzards. Every winter he used to go down to Lamjung to trade and buy rice, and in summer he would make a trip to Nar to barter dried cheese for buckwheat brought up from Manang. Now, however, his sons did his trading for him. Tashi's travelling days were over. The world beyond Kyang and the small village of Phu no longer held any attraction or meaning for him, and he was quite content to spend the rest of his life herding his sheep and goats and devoting more time to the religious observances that he hoped would bring him a good rebirth.

Wispy clouds converged over Kyang and the temperature abruptly dropped 20 degrees. Sleet began to fall. In the late afternoon Tashi left the house and walked down to the edge of the ravine above the Phu river. Throwing back his head, he delivered a long, ululating cry that rebounded hollowly from the cliff—a signal to his children that it was time to drive the flocks home. An answering call from his son and daughter rang across the valley. Minutes later, Tashi's flocks bounded down the pasture in trickles that merged into streams and finally swelled into a river of jostling, bleating animals, followed by two human dots. Without waiting for them to reach him, Tashi turned homewards. On the way, he found a large, flat rock that could be used for roofing. After trying unsuccessfully to break it with a stone, he hoisted it on to his back and bore it home in one piece.

The sun had slipped below the mountains by the time Dorje and Kamsum emerged from the ravine. Tashi told

This engagingly impressionistic map of the Nar-Phu valley, labelled in a mixture of Tibetan, Nepali and English, was drawn for the Time-Life team by Ang Nuri, the head Sherpa on the expedition. Their camp is shown above Nar (foreground); paths are marked in red and include most of the route to Phu (above, right).

more than a week longer, our homeward journey would become a dismal slog along dripping trails infested with leeches.

The news of the *drokpas* living near Phu solved the problem. To meet these permanent nomads would be even more intriguing than staying at the villagers' summer camps. We had in any case planned to travel to the end of the valley to see how Phu compared with Nar, and we decided to combine our expedition with a visit to the nearby *drokpa* camps.

We were sorry to leave Nar when we did because, with the hard work of planting over, a holiday atmosphere pervaded the village. As we packed up the tents, some of the young men were holding impromptu horse races above our camp, thundering over the close-cropped turf on sturdy ponies decked out in plumes and bright Tibetan rugs. The time for the villagers to relax together was all too brief. In a matter of weeks, many would leave with their herds for the high pastures; others would depart for Chame and Manang to trade butter and cheese for grain. As the summer wore on, the village of Nar would become half empty.

Since all but 10 of our porters had been paid off when we reached Nar, we had to hire a dozen girls to help carry our gear to Phu; none of the men volunteered. With complete lack of chivalry, our regular porters—some of whom were badly hungover from a night of revelry—gave the girls the heaviest loads. Amid shrill recriminations from the girls, we said our farewells to the villagers and, with reckless promises to return soon, we set off. It was good to be on the move again—to walk down through the warm updraft into the valley, where the birches had at last, grudgingly, unfurled their leaves. We crossed the bridge over the Nar river gorge and turned north for Phu, following a path normally taken only by the inhabitants of the two villages and occasional traders. Below us, the sides of the valley plunged down to the bed of the river, then rose in giant steps that were inscribed with loops and whorls where seams of quartz had been contorted by the squeezing-up of the Himalayas millions of years ago.

In mid-afternoon we came to Chaku, Nar's most northerly winter settlement, where a few fields were already green with barley. Many of Chaku's houses, like those at Meta, were old and dilapidated, and some had half-collapsed into the gorge because landslides had undermined their foundations; but in the centre stood a neat, military-looking row of much newer dwellings in good repair. Charlotte, who had already visited Chaku with a girl from Nar, explained that these houses had been built and occupied until a few years ago by refugees from the eastern Tibetan province of Kham.

Like the nomads, the Khambas had left their homeland as a result of the Chinese invasion. Living in the borderlands between Tibet and China, astride the main caravan routes, many of the Khambas lived by brigandage. When the Chinese arrived, they turned their banditry techniques against the advancing troops; but eventually they were forced to retreat west. From strongholds in Mustang, some Khambas moved south into the Nar-Phu valley. They settled at Chaku in the early 1960s, built new houses and created

Flat-roofed houses, built several storeys
high to save ground space, spill down the
steep hilltop on which Phu is perched. The
larger roofs are communal spots where
villagers gather to chat and work.

fields on previously uncultivated land, which they planted with barley and buckwheat. They shared the crops with the Nar landowners and bought yaks, butter and skins from Nar. Two Khambas, according to Charlotte's companion, had married local girls. Had they been allowed to remain, the refugees would probably have been absorbed into the societies of Nar and Phu—just as they have in the Sherpa region, where a young Khamba immigrant called Tenzing became the first man to set foot on the summit of Everest, and so made the name of his adopted people known to the world.

But the Nepalese Government was embarrassed by the presence of these anti-Chinese settlers in its sensitive border areas and in the mid-1970s the army was sent into the Nar-Phu valley to disperse the Khambas. Some went to Kathmandu, others to Pokhara. The villagers of Nar did not continue to cultivate the Khambas' fields and when we passed through Chaku, we saw that the land had reverted to pasture. An hour's walk from Chaku, we climbed a hill and stood looking down at Kyang, Phu's winter settlement, which sat in lonely isolation in a great bowl of mountains. We camped overnight on the turf surrounding the huddle of houses.

After Kyang there were no more trees; the great ranges behind us had robbed the air of its moisture, and we were now entering the cold arid zone that extends right across Tibet. The path dived down into the river gorge, sometimes dipping below the level of the stream where the current had piled up banks of rock. We crossed several wooden bridges that, Yonden told us, would be dismantled whenever the river flooded to prevent them being swept away: wood was an extremely precious commodity in Phu territory. When the bridges were removed, travellers had to take a lengthy alternative route, climbing the dizzying walls of the gorge to cross at one of the higher bridges that were left permanently in place.

Ahead of us, the river vanished into shadows where the opposite walls of the gorge almost met. The trail began to climb, zig-zagging up a staircase carved out of rock, sometimes hanging over thin air where gulleys had been bridged with tree trunks. At the top, a narrow gateway crowned with three small *chortens* guarded the approach to Phu. Beyond the gate, the path began a gentle descent; in places it was only inches wide, and the stream's distant murmur was an eloquent reminder of how far I would fall if I slipped.

A little farther upstream, the valley branched. The main arm continued north past a high crystalline peak towards Tibet—less than five miles away as the lammergeier flies, but two days' walk over the pass by which the fleeing *drokpas* had originally entered the Nar-Phu valley. The side valley climbed to the east. It was here that the *drokpas* had their encampments. A moment later, I saw Phu itself, tucked away in a fold of the mountains on the western side of the Phu river.

The village looked like a tiny fortress-citadel. For defence against bandits and to avoid wasting a single square foot of scarce arable land, it had been built on a 100-foot rock outcrop that fell sheer to the banks of the river. Most of Phu's 38 houses clustered on top of the outcrop or clung to its sides like swallows' nests; but a few spilled over a neck of land that joined the mountain behind the village. Here, on a flat rooftop, our tents were pitched.

In the afternoon, I climbed the mountain behind our camp. A gritty, nerve-fraying wind had sprung up as cold air from the distant snowfields rushed down to fill the partial vacuum created by warm air rising from the valleys. More than a thousand feet above the village, the wind rattled the bleached branches of thorn bushes and sent dust-devils spinning away over fields of shale split by sun and frost.

From where I stood, I had a bird's-eye view of the village and its setting. Several hundred feet above Phu, a few families were ploughing fields so steep that I held my breath each time a team turned at the top of a furrow, convinced that the yaks would lose their balance and topple backwards on the man straining to hang on to the plough. Although Phu was about a thousand feet lower than Nar, the land was considerably more arid and rocky. The valley bottom was narrow and steep-sided, and most of the fields were scattered in little pockets along the banks of the stream and in sheltered gulleys and hollows high on the mountain slopes—wherever there was a trickle of water to give life to the seed.

On the other side of the valley, tiny figures were inching along a trail towards the north, where Phu's main yak pastures and summer settlements lay. Above the trail, on a high bluff that commanded a fine view of the glittering peak to the north, stood Phu's main religious centre, the Tashi Gompa. Such sites are deliberately chosen: *gompa* means "a solitary place", where priests and monks can meditate without distractions. But the Tashi Gompa was also a reassuring symbol of protection, for the villagers had only to look across the valley to see its prayer flags whipping and cracking in the wind, offering defiance to invisible foes at the four corners of the horizon.

I had already heard about the temple from Nyendrak Singe, the head lama in Nar, whose eight-year-old grandson had been sent there to train as a lama. It sounded a much more formal place than the main temple in Nar where the head lama went every day but no one resided permanently; here at Phu there were several resident lamas, three of whom had been ordained. Nyendrak Singe had told me that the head lama of the Tashi Gompa was a Tibetan—another refugee from Kham. I was curious to know how he had obtained this exalted position and intended to visit him during our few days in Phu.

I came down from the mountain and set out to explore the crowded heart of Phu, entering the main village through a door that, in bygone days when Tibetan brigands menaced the valley, used to be shut and locked each evening. Because building space was so limited, many of the houses stood four storeys high, with one family occupying the lower floors and another the upper levels. I threaded my way through tiny alleyways, emerging into courtyards where men and women sat busily threshing grain, weaving blankets and making boots. I stopped to talk to some of them as they worked, and found them as lively, friendly and cheerful as the people in Nar—more so, if one considered the comparative harshness of their surroundings and the even greater paucity of their resources. One villager after another told me, uncomplainingly, how hard the fields were to work—potatoes would not grow, and though many barley seeds were planted, there was almost no return. The winters were so bad, they told me, that nobody stayed in the village; old people who could not walk were carried to Kyang. But when I asked them why, if things were so hard, they did not leave, they laughed. "This is the home of our ancestors. We would not want to abandon it," they said.

In the late afternoon, when the wind had died and the golden light of the westering sun transformed the village into a fairy-tale castle, everybody—men, women and children—collected on the west-facing terraces and rooftops opposite our camp to gossip and work. Then gradually, as the sun went down, they returned to their homes. The murmur of voices stilled; from every house rose the smoke of cooking fires. A chill gripped the valley. Over the eastern peaks, the full moon—a familiar object in an unfamiliar world—rose to turn the landscape black and silver. The inky spaces of the sky were knitted together with stars, and in the clear desert air I saw something I have never experienced under the murky skies of my own country: the constellations shifting their positions as the earth turned in space. A shooting star curved through the night like the shining tip of a scimitar, and vanished.

Next day, we walked up to the Tashi Gompa to seek an audience with the head lama. In a walled compound adjoining the building, a young man was teaching four small boys to recite texts. Their tutor introduced himself as the son of Lama Sonam, the head lama. He told us that three of the novices were from Phu; the fourth was the grandson of Nyendrak Singe, who after three years would return to Nar to be initiated into the village's rites and observances, ready to take on the inherited position of head lama on his grandfather's death. Before taking us to see his father, Lama Sonam's son invited us to look round the temple. At the door, he politely asked us to remove our shoes. He then ushered us into a large chamber which was decorated with newly painted frescoes and hung with paintings on silk banners. All of these, he told us proudly, were his father's work. The paintings, of Buddhas, gods and scenes from Buddhist mythology, were skilfully executed, but were rather garish. After looking round, we were led to the temple annexe, where the young man's wife served us tea.

My meeting with the head lama took place in his chamber above the main temple. On a low throne beside one wall of the dimly lit room, Lama Sonam sat idly spinning a prayer wheel. He must have been about 50, but he had a bland, curiously ageless face. He answered my questions readily enough, but in a disconcertingly distant manner that seemed to verge on boredom.

He told me that he had left Tibet more than 20 years before. As a young man, he had attended one of the big monastic colleges in Kham, where he had learnt to paint; then he had joined a large monastery near Lhasa. When the Chinese occupied Tibet, he had fled his homeland. Travelling with a large group of *drokpas*, he had come to Phu and had stayed for a short time; but then he had moved down to Manang to become a lama at Braga Gompa.

Three years later, a deputation of villagers from Phu had come to tell him that their head lama had died, and to invite him to take his place. There were

Swollen by melting snow during the spring thaw, the Phu river rushes beneath one of the village's three water mills, driving the millstones used to grind barley into flour. Downstream, garments have been anchored with rocks and left to soak in the clear water.

After her laborious descent from Phu village (top), a woman drinks from the river before resuming her journey to the pastures to collect dung for fuel.

several reasons for the villagers' choosing Lama Sonam, a stranger, to be their head lama. During his brief stay in Phu, they had been impressed by his skills as an artist: the Tashi Gompa at that time was neglected and in need of decoration. Just as important, Lama Sonam was prepared to be resident in the temple all the year round, even during the bitter winters when everyone else left the village for lower and milder altitudes. In the past, there had been thefts from the temple; the presence of a guardian meant that sacred objects and other valuables would be safe there.

The head lama told me that his son's wife, who had given me tea that morning, was the daughter of one of the *drokpa* families living near Phu. It seemed natural to ask whether he took a special interest in the welfare of the nomads, his compatriots. But he seemed surprised and irritated by the question; he would not be drawn. The interview was obviously over.

Not only the head lama but the other villagers too had been uncommunicative about the *drokpas*. Beyond their trading relations, the nomads seemed to impinge little on the lives of Phu people. The villagers' silence only increased my curiosity about their tent-dwelling neighbours, and I arranged to set off for the camps the next morning with Nik, Yonden and two of the Sherpas, while Christoph and Charlotte remained behind in the village.

We were woken before dawn by the shouts of women in the surrounding houses, bidding "Good morning" to their neighbours in the main village 70 yards away. The stars paled and went out, and at 6 a.m. precisely, two grinning Sherpas stuck their heads through the flap of my tent, greeted me cheerfully and handed me my breakfast of rice pudding.

It was a perfect day for hard walking. We crossed the Phu river, where women with baskets of barley were waiting for the rising sun to revive the stream with enough meltwater to drive the village water mills, then climbed gradually into the broad mouth of the valley that led to the east. We followed narrow sheep trails that meandered between lichen-covered rocks and shrubs whose crushed leaves released a scent of strawberries. Up here, the same wind that plagued Phu with clouds of choking dust blew fresh and clean, carrying flocks of tiny birds to their breeding grounds in Tibet. We were not the only people in the valley. For an hour, we fell in behind a herd of yaks being driven to pasture, and several times we met girls carrying baskets of sun-dried dung back to the village. At 14,000 feet we stopped to rest. Ahead of us, the valley broadened out into a shallow, rocky bowl. Cold blue snow-fields rose in deceptively gentle curves to meet a great pyramid of ice-armoured rock trailing banners of cloud. While the Sherpas collected fuel to make tea, Yonden climbed the hillside to search out the nomads' tents. Some 15 minutes later he reappeared as a speck against the sky, waving his hand towards a point on the northern rim of the valley. Quickly finishing our tea, we followed the direction he had indicated.

The tent lay like a giant bat among a circle of rocks. About six feet high and 20 feet square, with a gently pitched roof and sloping sides, it was made of peat-coloured yak hair. Its base was anchored by 20 wooden pegs, but the

Dwarfed by the sheer cliff face above and below them, three villagers negotiate a narrow and dangerous trail cut in the rock that leads from Phu to the summer pastures north of the village. The smooth gully running down the slope behind them is the result of a landslide—only one of the many hazards that confront mountain travellers.

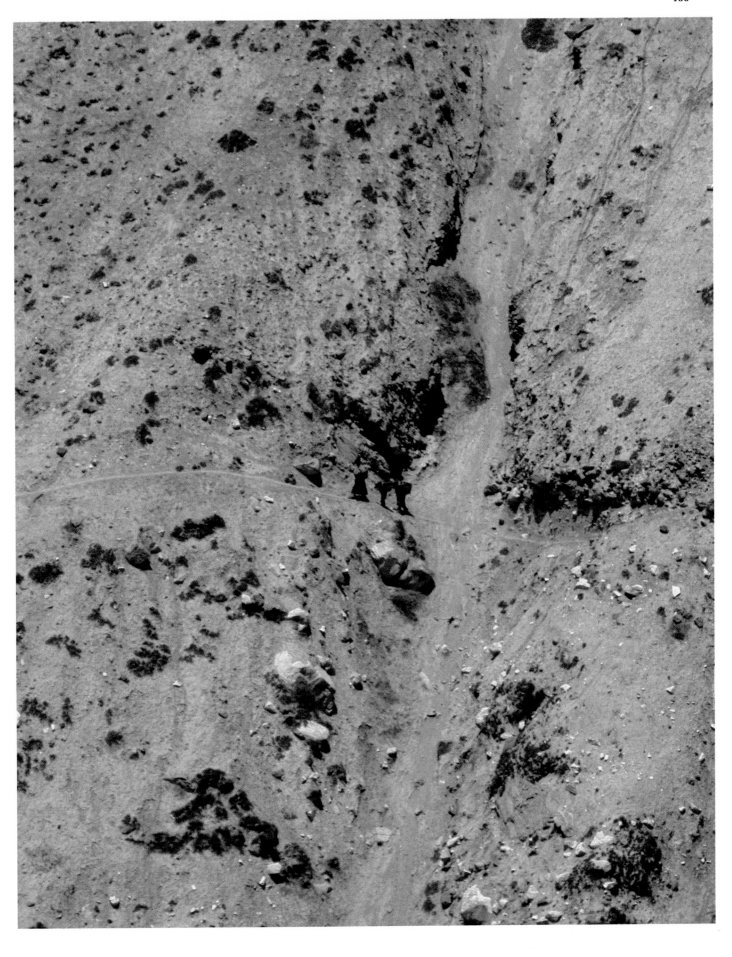

main support was supplied by two internal props and eight guy-ropes—one at each corner of the tent and one mid-way down each side—that were stretched taut over external props and securely tied to rocks about 10 feet from the tent. Like many strictly utilitarian objects, it was a beautiful and deceptively simple structure; the small pitch of the roof, the low profile and the system of angled guys were perfectly designed to withstand the gales and blizzards of the Tibetan Plateau.

A dog yapped at our sudden intrusion. As a guard dog, the animal failed to live up to the fearsome description I had been given by Tashi Wangdi in Nar; it was an indeterminate kind of terrier of a size that could have inflicted no worse damage than a nipped ankle. Its yapping served some function, however, for, alerted by the racket, a man emerged from the tent and watched us approach. He was short and compact, with regular, rather Gallic features and a long pigtail that he wore pinned in an elaborate coil on the back of his head. Showing no surprise at our unexpected arrival, he pulled back the entrance flap of the tent and courteously ushered us into his home.

The interior was warm and airy, in striking contrast to the dark, cramped, stuffy—and dirty—houses of Nar and Phu. A dung fire glowed in a metal brazier on the central hearth, which was located directly under a horizontal vent that ran almost the length of the roof. Beside the fire, a woman with a careworn face held a small baby with one hand and stirred a pot of tea with the other. The man—the tentholder—joined his wife on the left side of the hearth, where the family had their sleeping area, and invited us to be seated opposite, in the place reserved for guests. We sat on a fine but faded Tibetan rug decorated with a swastika—a traditional motif—and I looked round the tent, taking stock. Dried dung and firewood filled one of the corners near the entrance; cooking utensils occupied another corner. Blankets, spare clothing and pieces of harness were stowed neatly on a low shelf of stones that ran round the interior of the tent. Directly opposite the entrance was a low stone altar where butter lamps burnt before framed, hand-tinted photographs of the Dalai Lama and the late lama of Braga Gompa.

I asked the nomad, whose name was Chorphel, how such a tent was constructed. He explained that it was sewn together from 18 panels of yak hair. It took a family three months to make a tent, but new ones were made only when a son got married and established his own tenthold. Existing tents were never discarded; instead, worn and frayed sections were renewed piece by piece. Each year, Chorphel explained, one or two new panels were woven and incorporated into the centre of the roof, replacing existing panels that were then shifted outwards to become the sides. However many new panels were added, the same number of panels were discarded from the base of the tent, which rotted and frayed more quickly than the upper portions. Theoretically, a *drokpa* tent is ageless; it has a kind of life of its own, like an animal that sloughs off its old, dead skin.

Chorphel told me that the tent would remain waterproof even if it rained for six days; and he demonstrated how the door and roof vent could be closed by a system of horn toggles and leather loops. I found his claim hard to

Tent-Dwelling Herdsmen from Tibet

Less than five miles south of the Tibetan border, in a valley east of Phu, dwells a scattering of nomadic families whose way of life is even more precarious than that of the villagers of Nar and Phu. Refugees who fled Tibet after the Chinese takeover in 1959, they own no land, but are allowed to graze their small flocks of sheep and goats on Phu territory in return for an annual rent. Every three or four months, after the grazing lands in their immediate vicinity are exhausted, the nomads move off in search of un-cropped pastures elsewhere in the valley.

The nomads live in tents throughout the year, protected from the bitter Himalayan climate by a single layer of woven yak hair. These seemingly inadequate shelters are, in fact, warm and waterproof, and made so expertly they last a lifetime. Each one consists of 15 or more panels stitched together; individual panels are replaced as they become worn.

The tents are pitched on a circle of stone slabs painstakingly laid out by the nomads. Inside, the accommodation is surprisingly spacious, easily holding a family of six. Separate areas for eating, sleeping and receiving guests are furnished with rugs and blankets.

With its flagged floor and domestic clutter, an established camp gives the impression of permanence—but it can be dismantled easily and quickly. The tent and its contents are loaded on to pack-horses and within two hours the place is deserted. Only the paved site remains, to be used again and again by its builders and by the other nomad families.

An elderly nomad and his bespectacled wife relax with their family outside their tent, which is secured by ropes attached to a circle of poles.

A stone floor built round an earthen hearth marks the site of an abandoned nomad camp. The narrow ledge skirting the floor was used to store domestic utensils; the low wall that partly encompasses the site served to exclude draughts by bridging the gap between the tent base and the ground.

A nomad family prepares for a meal in their shadowy tent. A vent above them admits light and allows smoke to escape. Behind them is a tiny altar.

believe, since the weave of the fabric was so loose that I could see the surrounding mountains through the walls—a beautiful, textured effect, like a
landscape painted in glowing oils that in the course of time have worn away
until the canvas shows through. But Chorphel explained that the yak hair
swelled when wet, effectively sealing the holes. I wondered why the people
of Nar and Phu, who use identical tents in the high summer pastures, did not
live permanently in such practical shelters, which are dry and warm for the
winter, yet airy in hot weather, and infinitely superior to our own flimsy
camping tents in which we froze by night and baked by day.

On learning that we would be spending the night beside his tent, Chorphel
invited us to share a meal at his hearth. While we ate, he told me why he had
come to Phu from his home in Hapchin, 10 days' walk north of the border.
His father, now dead, had been a lama who fled to Nepal because he feared
that he might suffer religious persecution under the Chinese. A year later,
after the invaders had taken the family herd, Chorphel, his wife and two
daughters followed the lama into exile. Chorphel had managed to save a few
sheep and seven yaks, which he drove to Phu with the idea of building up a
new herd. But he found that there were about 40 refugee families already
camping in Phu territory. There was nowhere for him to graze his animals,
and he was forced to sell them and move south. He found work as a field
hand in Manang. The other refugee families were moved on, and most of
them also settled in Manang. But Chorphel missed the nomad way of life.
After two years, with the money he had saved from his wages and the sale of
his animals, he bought a small flock of sheep and goats and asked the Phu
council if he could return to their territory. In agreeing to his request, the villagers may have been swayed by the representations of their head lama; for
Chorphel turned out to be the nomad whose youngest daughter was married

Slabs of rock supported by stones make a
rugged kennel for a mastiff that belongs to a
nomad family. Once kept to warn of the
approach of raiding bandits, these fierce
dogs now serve only to protect the family's
livestock from predatory animals.

to the lama's son. The village council had also agreed to individual requests from three other nomad families who wished to return to Phu territory.

Like the other nomad families, Chorphel paid a small annual fee to the village for his grazing rights. Since pasturage within the small valley occupied by the *drokpas* was limited, he was not allowed to keep yaks, which meant he had to buy yak hair from the villagers when he wanted to repair his tent. It cost 3,000 rupees to make a new tent, Chorphel told me—a little less than half the amount a villager might spend on building materials for a new house. To raise money to buy yak hair, as well as salt, rice and other essentials, he sold a few sheep and goats each year to the Manangbas and spent a few weeks in the autumn helping them bring in their harvest. His 70 sheep and 38 goats supplied most of the family's food; surplus milk was turned into butter and exchanged in Manang for buckwheat. Alone among the nomads, Chorphel grew his own barley. He owned three fields in Phu—an unusual concession to a recent immigrant with no clan connections in the village, and probably another benefit that he owed to his relative, the head lama.

Although they kept their camps some distance apart, the nomad families co-operated with one another in arranging their frequent moves to new pastures within the valley. The family at the far end of the valley owned six horses that were used as pack animals whenever a family moved camp. In winter, when the Phu villagers abandoned their houses to go to Kyang, the nomads moved to a disused settlement north of Phu, where they fed their animals on fodder collected during the summer. If the winter snows were so bad that the villagers were forced to abandon Phu, how did the nomads survive at even higher altitudes? Chorphel admitted that conditions were sometimes so bad that many of his sheep and goats perished, and he and his family were forced to take shelter in caves.

As we were talking, Chorphel's unmarried daughter and his eight-year-old son returned with the sheep and goats for the evening milking. The daughter, who was the mother of the baby that Chorphel's wife was cradling, came into the tent to boil a pot of water and then went outside with it. A few minutes later she returned with soaking hair that she dried by pulling the black tresses over her face, laying them on a carpet and beating them with a bundle of twigs. I was disconcerted to see that she was giving Nik and me long, suggestive looks from beneath the veil of hair. Yonden noticed the suggestive glances, too. He told me that the girl's baby had been fathered by a minor official in Chame.

Casual sexual encounters and illegitimate children are accepted by the Bhotia, but I could see that this young mother and the other unmarried children of the nomads faced a serious predicament. Confined to an isolated valley, owning no land, having no established connections with the villagers, how could they expect to find husbands and wives? Chorphel agreed that the marriage prospects of his children were not good. In Tibet, he would have arranged his children's marriages, but his own depleted economic position made it difficult to marry into Phu society. His son and daughter would be free to find their own mates. Perhaps they would marry *drokpa* refugees

who had settled in Manang and now worked as cultivators. But if they did that, they would have to abandon the nomad life.

"Why don't you return to Tibet?" I asked Chorphel. I tried to explain that the Chinese had been obliged to soften their policy of collectivization and allow the nomads to keep their own livestock. Nik added that the communists had moderated their campaign against religion and had invited the Dalai Lama to return. "When I was living in Manang," Chorphel said, "a friend visited Tibet and brought back news from my sister. She said that some *drokpas* still lived the nomadic life, but most of them worked in fields that the Chinese had forced them to cultivate on the old pastures. My father's temple has been destroyed. Without sheep and religion, there is nothing for me."

Snow was falling when we woke next morning. Inside his tent, Chorphel was reciting a sacred text, sometimes leafing back through the pages to re-read a section as if to wring more meaning and merit from the words. We left him sitting before the altar, bathed in the soft glow of guttering butter lamps, and continued our journey to the most distant nomad camp. An hour later, with my altimeter reading 14,700 feet, we breasted a low rise and saw that the valley did not end at the pyramid-shaped mountain that loomed a mile farther to the east, but fell away into a gaping abyss where cloud wraiths seethed among ghostly turrets and pinnacles of ice. Down there was Tibet.

A horse whinnied close by. Looking in the direction of the sound, I saw the brightly coloured pennants that the nomads hang on their guy-ropes as prayer flags. A woman stood beside the tent, but it was the dog that claimed my attention. Standing as high as the woman's waist, with a heavy head, a shaggy black coat and a tail that curved over its back, it advanced on us with

Nanny goats that have been mustered for milking stand tethered to face one another in two interlocking rows (above, left). A woman stoops to collect the milk in the large curved horn of a wild yak (inset, above).

stiff-legged menace. Instinctively, we bunched closer together and stopped. The woman calmly surveyed us for a minute, then said something to the dog, which turned and allowed itself to be tied to a chain secured to a rough stone kennel about 40 yards from the tent. When I got closer, I realized that the mastiff was a handsome beast—rather like a Newfoundland. But its coat was bare in patches, and when it opened its mouth to snarl, I saw that its teeth were worn down. It was a very old dog, and although its hackles bristled as we walked past, it readily subsided into its kennel at the woman's command, obviously relieved that it was not being called upon to tear our throats out.

Three other people were descending to the camp carrying bundles of brushwood. In the centre was a tall man who walked with the bow-legged gait of a horseman; a small boy and girl were with him, and when they saw us, they reached up to take his hands. Dressed in an ankle-length coat of black, oiled sheepskin worn with the wool inside, the man had a striking, bandit's face adorned with a long, drooping moustache that reminded me of portraits of Genghis Khan. But when he got closer, I saw from his rheumy, downward-slanting eyes that he, too, was very old. Age had not diminished the pride he took in his appearance, however. His feet were shod in exquisitely patterned and coloured Tibetan boots with rakish, upturned toes. They had been made, he told us later, by his son-in-law, "the best boot-maker in Tibet." The nomad was 81; the woman and children were his daughter and grandchildren. Both his son-in-law and unmarried son were in Phu, he explained, attending a ceremony at one of the temples. Inside the tent, we met his wife, an 80-year-old matriarch with silver hair and blind eyes.

We had arrived in time to watch the morning milking. Taking the sheep and goats out of the pens one by one, the daughter tied them together in two rows facing each other, with a long rope passed around their necks. They were so closely packed together that a strange optical illusion was created; the head of each animal seemed to be growing out of the back of its opposite number and, to add to my confusion, it appeared to be growing backwards.

When all the animals were in line, with the sheep at one end and the goats at the other, the woman began milking them into a massive hollowed-out horn. I asked the nomad what animal it had come from, and he told me that it was the horn of a wild yak he had shot near his home on the Chang Thang, 15 days' journey to the north. And for the next half hour he regaled me with stories of hunting on the Tibetan plateau. Altogether, he had shot 30 wild yaks, he said. When he was a young man, he had used a matchlock—a long-barrelled gun fired by igniting the powder with a glowing match. Later, he had acquired a rifle. Remembering Yonden's story about the fierceness of wild yaks, I asked the nomad if such hunting was dangerous. His eyes lit up as he remembered his exploits. Oh yes, he replied. But he had always shot from a high vantage point, safe from the charge of a wounded animal. While the man spoke, his old wife sat counting her rosary, chuckling softly at her husband's enthusiastic reminiscences.

We talked for a little longer. At one point in the conversation, the nomad got up and sent a stone from a sling singing towards a horse that was coming

too close to the tent. When he sat down again, obviously pleased to have been able to demonstrate his marksmanship, I asked him how the *drokpas* differed from the villagers of Nar and Phu. Like us, he said, they are followers of the *dharma*, the Law of Buddha. He conceded that the villagers were good herdsmen, but boasted that his family had once owned as many animals as all the Phu herds put together. He was even more disparaging about the villagers' marriage customs. "They marry their own cousins," he said. Among the *drokpas*, he added, it was common for two brothers to share the same wife to prevent the family property being broken up. When I asked him how such arrangements worked, he told me that the husbands were rarely in the camp at the same time. "One man would be in the pastures with the wife, while the other was away trading. If husbands and wife were in the camp together, they always slept separately."

It was time to leave. The day was more than half gone, and we had arranged to be back in Phu that evening, which would be our last in the village. We said farewell and set off down the valley. When I turned round, the nomad was still watching us with his arm raised in salute—a solitary figure standing by a tent at the end of a valley that looked into Tibet.

Our departure from Phu was more formal than the leave-taking we had received in Nar. Some of the lamas and many of the villagers came to our camp to say goodbye. Then, ceremoniously, one lama presented each of us with a *kata*—a white scarf frequently exchanged between host and guest among the Bhotia. We left wearing the *katas* round our necks, accompanied by 10

Whirling his sling around his head, a nomad prepares to launch a stone to round up a group of horses. By landing the stone near the animals' feet, he will startle them into moving off in the desired direction.

Phu girls who had offered to help us carry our possessions down the valley as far as Chame. When we had walked a little way, I asked Yonden what the lama had said in farewell. "Go slowly." It was the same valediction given to us by the nomads when we had left their encampments.

And so, slowly, we went: down the rock staircase carved out of the mountain; through Kyang and Chaku and Meta; past the trail to the valley of Namya where the bells of the yaks would be chiming through the perpetual mists, to be answered by the cries of the herders; along the forest trails, now half-covered with bamboo and alive with flowers and birdsong. Just before we reached the hut where we had spent the first night in the valley, we came upon a column of about 50 Nar people who were carrying large sacks of rice from the lowlands back to their village. The next day, we heard the roar of the Marsyandi and arrived in Chame.

For days we had looked forward to our arrival in this administrative centre. We would enjoy a respite from our cook's limited menu; we could even drink cold beer, brought up the valley on the backs of porters and sold at a price that would not have disgraced a luxury hotel. But most of all we looked forward to bathing in the hot springs that welled out of the rocks just upstream of the village. In the weeks we had spent with the Bhotia, I had adopted their minimal washing habits. After eating, we went eagerly to the springs, followed by the 10 girls from Phu. In the first spring, a woman was washing her clothes; in the next, a Hindu couple sat naked, talking together with great dignity and not even deigning to look up when we passed. The third spring was free. Subjected to the critical gaze of the giggling girls, we dissolved the weeks of accumulated grime. We encouraged our audience to share the experience. They giggled even louder, but two girls decided to come down to the spring to join us and, chastely lifting their *chubas* just above the knee, daintily soaped their legs.

That evening, we sat eating and drinking round a heroic fire. One of the girls began to sing, another took up the refrain, then they linked arms round each other's waists, formed a line and began to dance. With shuffling steps, the girls moved first to one side, then to the other, ending each phrase with a gentle kicking movement. Some of the Sherpas joined them. They did not know the words of the song, but they knew the music and the steps. Backwards and forwards the line swayed in the firelight—men and women whose homes lay many days apart, whose speech and way of life were different, but who were linked by a common culture and tradition. Theirs was a medieval world where there were no machines and where all art, literature and knowledge were disseminated by priests. In their mountainous homeland, the supernatural still had the power to invade men's minds—yet my overwhelming impression was not of a race held in thrall by superstition. The picture of the Bhotia that I was taking back with me was one of a sturdy, practical and self-reliant group of people who had come to terms with their daunting environment and who, imperfectly but unquestioningly, followed the precepts of the compassionate Law of Buddha.

Bibliography

Bista, Dor Bahadur, *People of Nepal*. Ratna Pustak Bhandar, Kathmandu, 1967.

Ekvall, Robert B., "Some Aspects of Divination in Tibetan Society." *Ethnology*, Pittsburg, Vol. 2, 1963.

Ekvall, Robert B., *Fields on the Hoof: Nexus of Tibetan Nomadic Pastoralism*. Holt, Rinehart & Winston, New York & London, 1968.

Fürer-Haimendorf, Christoph von, *The Sherpas of Nepal*. John Murray, London, 1964.

Fürer-Haimendorf, Christoph von (editor), *Contributions to the Anthropology of Nepal*. Aris & Phillips, Warminster, 1974.

Fürer-Haimendorf, Christoph von, *Himalayan Traders*. John Murray, London, 1975.

Gurung, N. J., "An Introduction to the Socio-Economic Structure of Manang District." *Kailash – A Journal of Himalayan Studies*. Ratna Pustak Bhandar, Kathmandu, Vol. 4, No. 3, 1976.

Gurung, N. J., "An Ethnographic Note on Nar-Phu Valley." *Kailash – A Journal of Himalayan Studies*. Ratna Pustak Bhandar, Kathmandu, Vol. 5, No. 3, 1977.

Jest, Corneille, *Tarap: Une Vallée dans L'Himalaya*. Éditions du Seuil, Paris, 1974.

Jest, Corneille, *Dolpo: Communautés de Langue Tibétaine du Népal*. Éditions du Centre National de la Recherche Scientifique, Paris, 1975.

Karan, Pradyumna P., *Nepal: A Cultural and Physical Geography*. University of Kentucky Press, Lexington, 1960.

Matthiessen, Peter, *The Snow Leopard*. Chatto & Windus, London, 1979.

Ortner, Sherry B., *Sherpas Through Their Rituals*. Cambridge University Press, Cambridge, 1978.

Peissel, Michel, *Mustang*, Collins & Harvill Press, London, 1968.

Shakabpa, Tsepon W. D., *Tibet. A Political History*. Yale University Press, New Haven & London, 1967.

Snellgrove, David, *Himalayan Pilgrimage*. Bruno Cassirer, Oxford, 1961.

Snellgrove, David and Richardson, Hugh, *A Cultural History of Tibet*. Weidenfeld & Nicolson, London, 1968.

Stein, R. A., *Tibetan Civilisation*. Faber & Faber, London, 1972.

Tucci, Giuseppe, *The Religions of Tibet*. Routledge & Kegan Paul, London & Henley, 1980.

Waddell, L. Austine, *The Buddhism of Tibet*. W. H. Allen, London, 1895.

Zwalf, W., *Heritage of Tibet*. British Museum Publications, London, 1981.

Acknowledgements and Picture Credits

The members of the expedition express their profound gratitude to His Majesty King Birendra Bir Bikram Shah Deva for graciously permitting them to carry out research in the Nar region of the Manang District.

The author, photographer, consultants and editors of this book also wish to thank the following: Kamal Dos Adhikari, Home Ministry, Kathmandu; Ang Nuri and the Sherpas of Sherpa Co-operative, Kathmandu; Lain Singh Bangdel, Chancellor, Royal Nepal Academy, Kathmandu; Professor Dor Bahadur Bista, Tribhuvan University, Kathmandu; Mike Brown, London; Mike Cheney, Kathmandu; Jim Edwards, Kathmandu; Dr. Harka B. Gurung, Kathmandu; Prema Tsering Gurung, Manang; Elizabeth Hawley, Kathmandu; Michael MacCarthy-Morrogh, London; Library of the Museum of Mankind, London; Colonel J. Roberts, Kathmandu; Narayan Prasad Shrestha, Palace Secretariat, Kathmandu; Lisa van Gruisen, Kathmandu.

The sources for the pictures in this book are listed on the right. Credits for each of the photographers and illustrators are listed by page number in sequence; where necessary, the locations of pictures within pages are also indicated—separated from page numbers by dashes.

All photographs by Nik Wheeler, Black Star, except: Pamela Bellwood, 4—second from top; Windsor Chorlton, 160; Paul Fox, 4—third from top; Lafayette Studio, London, 4—bottom; Alan Lothian, 4—top.

Illustrations (alphabetically): Maps by Terry Allen and Nicholas Skelton for Creative Cartography Ltd., 20-21. Front end-paper map by Engineering Surveys Reproduction Ltd. Map by Ang Nuri, Kathmandu, 147.

Index